TOWN PLAN ATLAS BRITAIN

BARTHOLOMEW

CONTENTS

motorway with junction
autoroute et accès
Autobahn mit Kreuzung
autostrada con stazione

motorway under construction/projected
autoroute en construction/en projet
Autobahn im Bau/geplant
autostrada in costruzione/in progetto

trunk road
grand itinéraire
Fernverkehrstraße
Strada di grande comunicazione

main road
route principale
Hauptstraße
strada principale

other roads
autres routes
ubrige Straßen
altre Strade

A1   M1   T9   **road numbering**
B6211   L29   numérotage des routes
Straßennumerierung
numerazione delle strade

car ferry
bac pour autos
Autofähre
autotraghetto

railway
chemin de fer
Eisenbahn
ferrovia

airport
aéroport
Flughafen
aeroporto

© John Bartholomew & Son Ltd., Edinburgh
Printed and Published in Great Britain by
John Bartholomew & Son Ltd. 1973
ISBN   085152 817 1

We would be glad to have our attention drawn to
any changes which may have taken place between
the preparation and publication.

5046

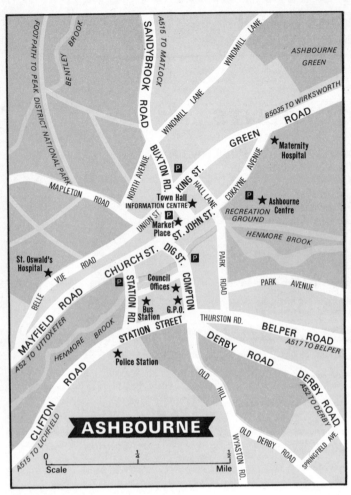

ASHBOURNE

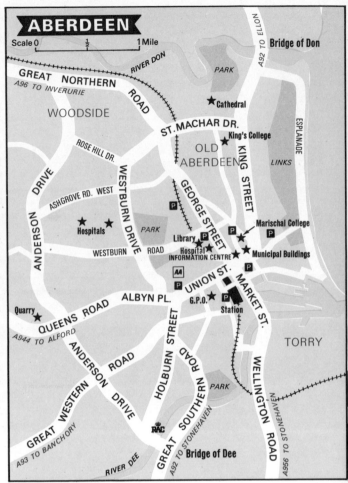

ABERDEEN

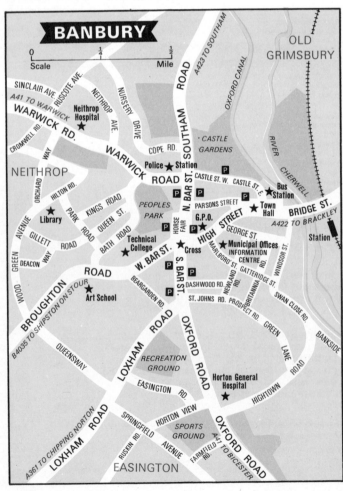

BANBURY

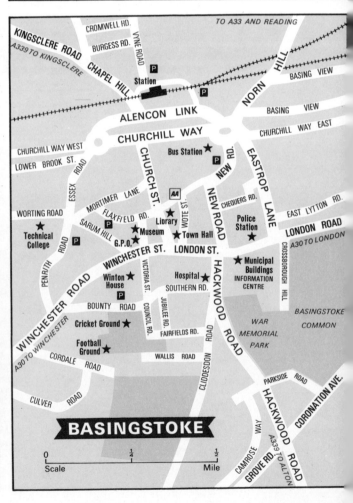

BASINGSTOKE

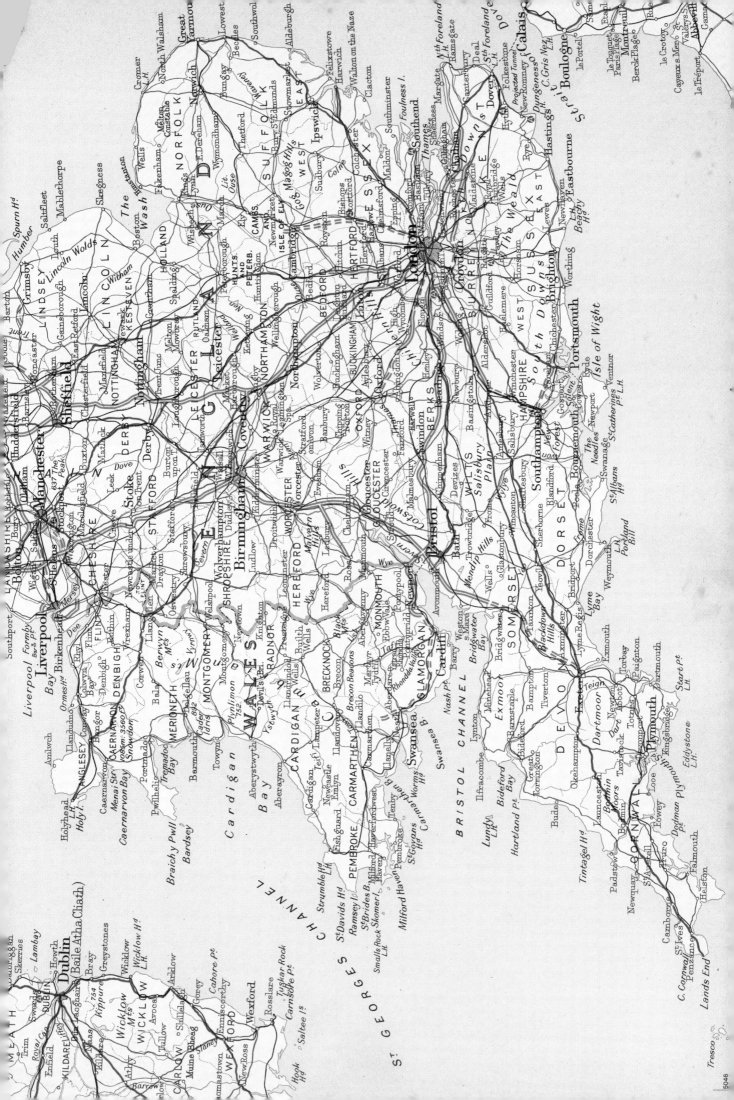

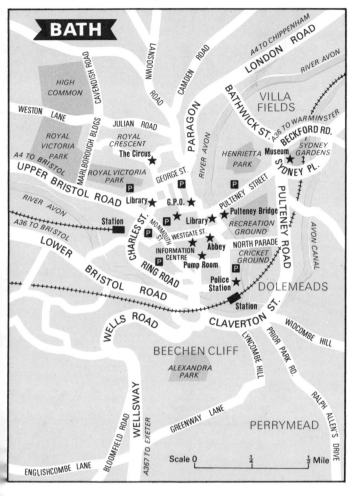

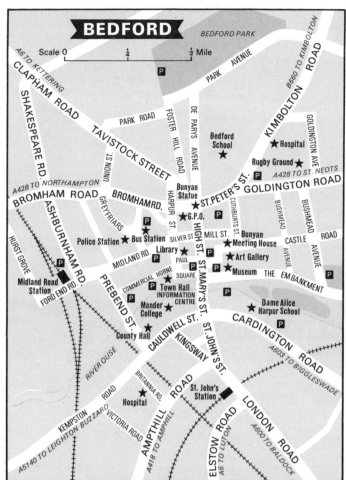

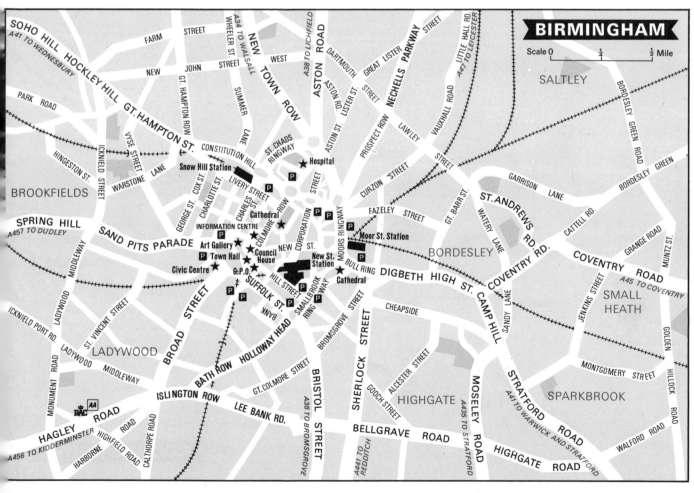

4

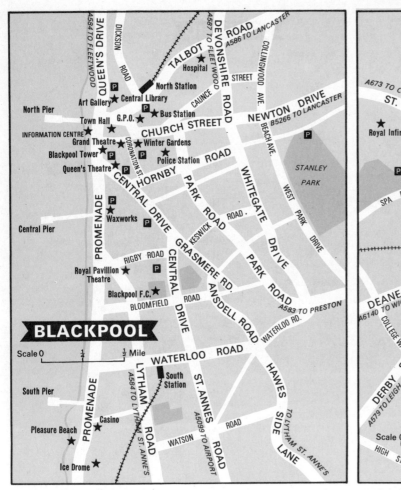

BLACKPOOL

Hospital
North Station
Art Gallery
Central Library
North Pier
Town Hall
G.P.O.
Bus Station
INFORMATION CENTRE
CHURCH STREET
Grand Theatre
Winter Gardens
Blackpool Tower
Police Station
Queen's Theatre
Waxworks
Central Pier
Royal Pavillion Theatre
Blackpool F.C.
BLOOMFIELD
Scale 0 ¼ ½ Mile
South Station
South Pier
Casino
Pleasure Beach
Ice Drome

DICKSON ROAD
QUEEN'S DRIVE
A584 TO FLEETWOOD
DEVONSHIRE ROAD
A587 TO FLEETWOOD
TALBOT ROAD
A586 TO LANCASTER
COLLINGWOOD AVE.
STREET
CAUNCE
NEWTON DRIVE
B5266 TO LANCASTER
BEACH AVE.
HORNBY ROAD
CORONATION ST.
HORNBY
CENTRAL DRIVE
PARK ROAD
KESWICK ROAD
GRASMERE RD.
ANSDELL ROAD
PROMENADE
RIGBY ROAD
CENTRAL DRIVE
ROAD
WHITEGATE DRIVE
WEST PARK DRIVE
STANLEY PARK
PARK ROAD
WATERLOO RD.
A583 TO PRESTON
WATERLOO ROAD
LYTHAM ROAD
A584 TO LYTHAM ST. ANNE'S
ST. ANNES ROAD
HAWES SIDE LANE
TO LYTHAM ST. ANNE'S
WATSON ROAD
A5099 TO AIRPORT
PROMENADE

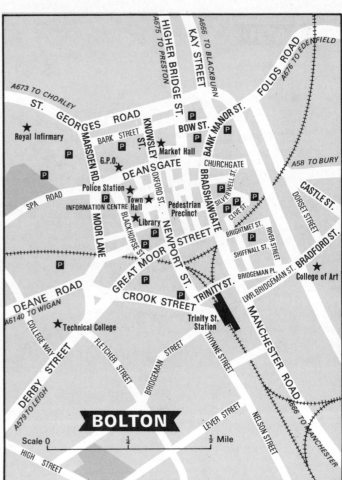

BOLTON

Royal Infirmary
Market Hall
G.P.O.
DEANSGATE
Police Station
Town Hall
INFORMATION CENTRE
Library
Pedestrian Precinct
Trinity St. Station
Technical College
CROOK STREET
Scale 0 ¼ ½ Mile
College of Art

A673 TO CHORLEY
A675 TO PRESTON
HIGHER BRIDGE ST.
KAY STREET
A666 TO BLACKBURN
FOLDS ROAD
A676 TO EDENFIELD
ST. GEORGES ROAD
MARSDEN RD.
BARK STREET
KNOWSLEY ST.
BOW ST.
BANK MANOR ST.
CHURCHGATE
A58 TO BURY
OXFORD ST.
BRADSHAWGATE
SILVERWELL ST.
CLIVE ST.
CASTLE ST.
DURSET STREET
BRIGHTMET ST.
MOOR LANE
BLACKHORSE ST.
NEWPORT ST.
GREAT MOOR STREET
SHIFFNALL ST.
RIVER STREET
BRADFORD ST.
DEANE ROAD
A6140 TO WIGAN
TRINITY ST.
BRIDGEMAN PL.
LWR.BRIDGEMAN ST.
SPA ROAD
DERBY STREET
A579 TO LEIGH
COLLEGE WAY
FLETCHER STREET
BRIDGEMAN STREET
THYNNE STREET
MANCHESTER ROAD
A666 TO MANCHESTER
LEVER STREET
NELSON STREET
HIGH STREET

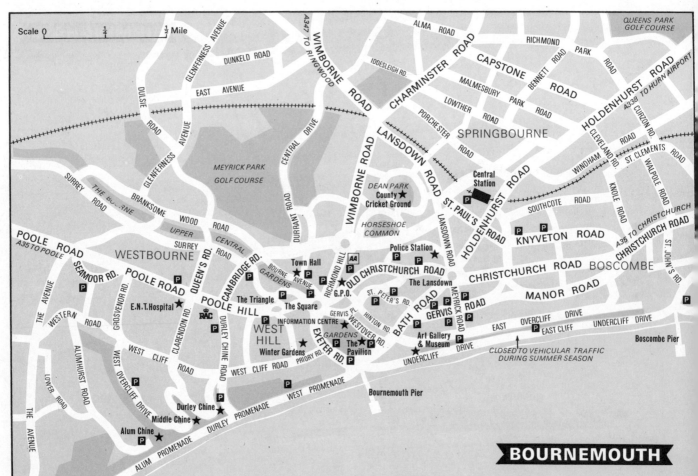

BOURNEMOUTH

Scale 0 ¼ ½ Mile
QUEENS PARK GOLF COURSE
ALMA ROAD
RICHMOND PARK ROAD
GLENEFERNESS AVENUE
DUNKELD ROAD
EAST AVENUE
IDDESLEIGH RD.
CHARMINSTER ROAD
CAPSTONE ROAD
BENNETT ROAD
HOLDENHURST ROAD
A338 TO HURN AIRPORT
A347 TO RINGWOOD
WIMBORNE ROAD
MALMESBURY PARK ROAD
LOWTHER ROAD
SPRINGBOURNE
CLEVELAND RD.
CURZON RD.
ST. CLEMENTS ROAD
DULSIE ROAD
AVENUE
GLENEFERNESS
CENTRAL DRIVE
LANSDOWN ROAD
PORCHESTER ROAD
WINDHAM ROAD
WALPOLE ROAD
MEYRICK PARK GOLF COURSE
DEAN PARK
County Cricket Ground
Central Station
KNOLE ROAD
A35 TO CHRISTCHURCH
SURREY ROAD
THE BOURNE
BRANKSOME
WIMBORNE ROAD
HORSESHOE COMMON
ST. PAUL'S ROAD
SOUTHCOTE ROAD
POOLE ROAD
A35 TO POOLE
WOOD ROAD
UPPER CENTRAL ROAD
SURREY ROAD
Town Hall
AA
Police Station
HOLDENHURST ROAD
KNYVETON ROAD
CHRISTCHURCH ROAD
ST. JOHN'S RD.
WESTBOURNE
SEAMOOR RD.
POOLE ROAD
QUEEN'S RD.
CAMBRIDGE RD.
BOURNE GARDENS
RICHMOND HILL
OLD CHRISTCHURCH ROAD
The Lansdown
CHRISTCHURCH ROAD
BOSCOMBE
GROSVENOR RD.
POOLE HILL
The Triangle
The Square
G.P.O.
ST. PETER'S RD.
BATH ROAD
GERVIS ROAD
MEYRICK ROAD
MANOR ROAD
THE AVENUE
WESTERN ROAD
E.N.T.Hospital
RAC
CLARENDON RD.
DURLEY CHINE ROAD
WEST HILL
GERVIS PL.
HINTON RD.
WESTOVER RD.
INFORMATION CENTRE
Winter Gardens
The Pavilion
Gardens
EXETER RD.
Art Gallery & Museum
EAST OVERCLIFF DRIVE
EAST CLIFF
UNDERCLIFF DRIVE
Boscombe Pier
ALUMHURST ROAD
WEST CLIFF ROAD
WEST CLIFF ROAD
PRIORY ROAD
UNDERCLIFF DRIVE
CLOSED TO VEHICULAR TRAFFIC DURING SUMMER SEASON
LOWER ROAD
WEST OVERCLIFF DRIVE
Durley Chine
Middle Chine
Alum Chine
WEST PROMENADE
ALUM PROMENADE
DURLEY PROMENADE
Bournemouth Pier
THE AVENUE

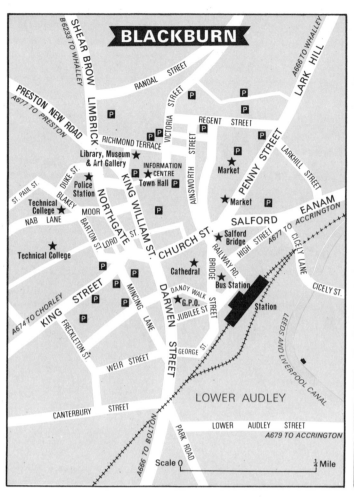

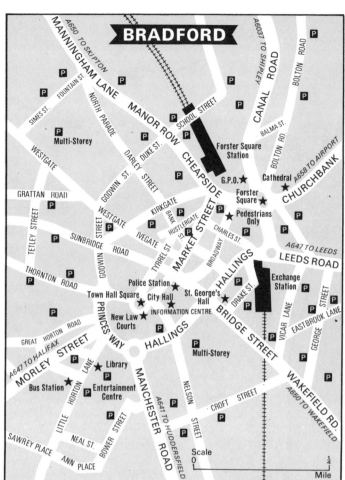

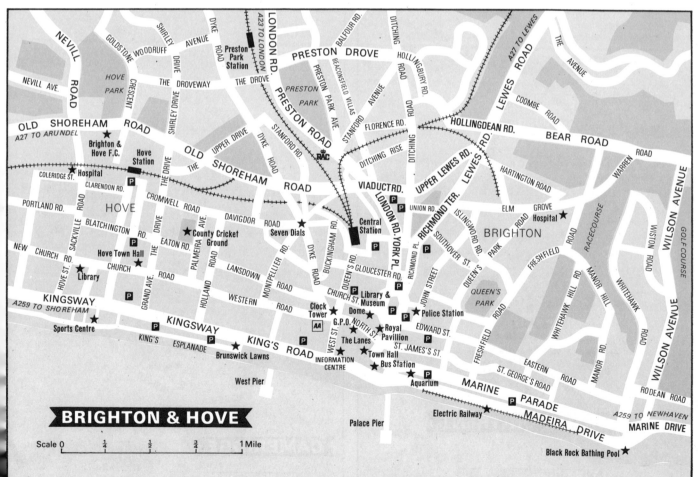

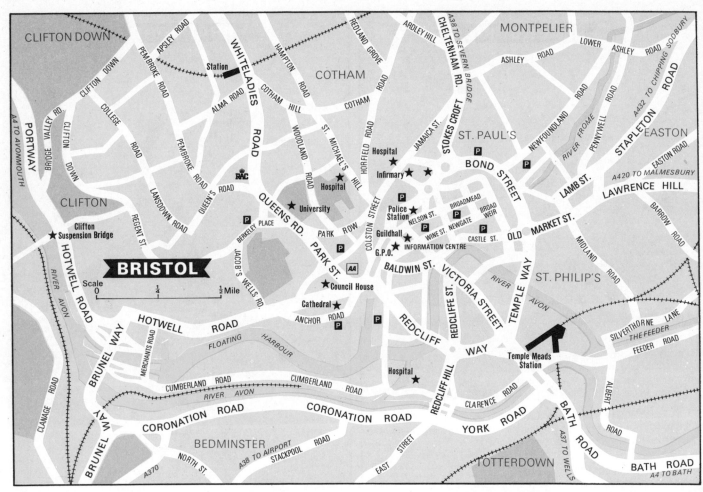

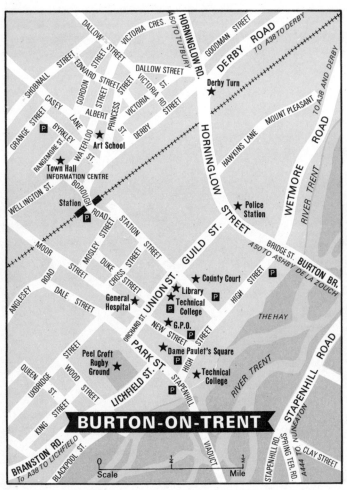

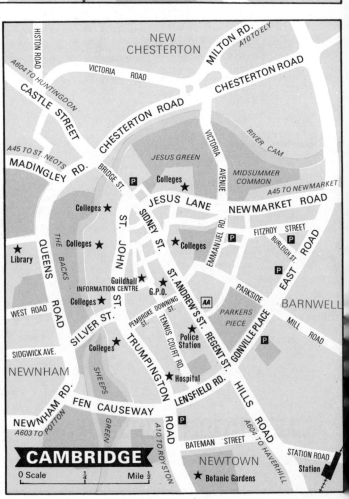

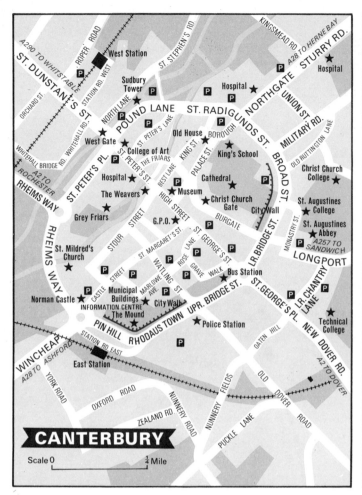

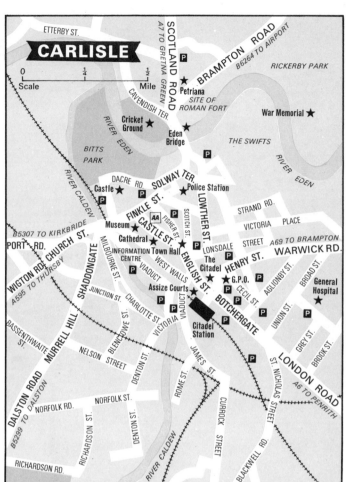

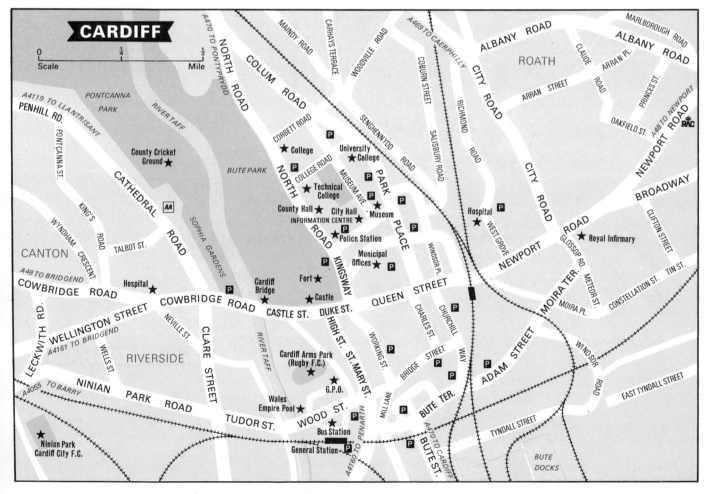

8

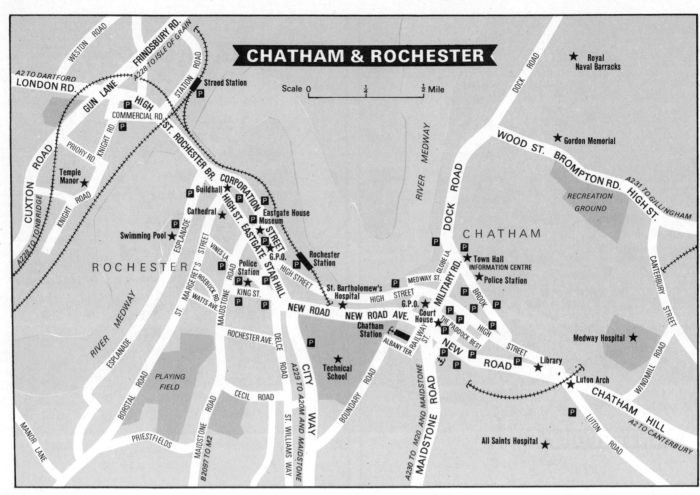

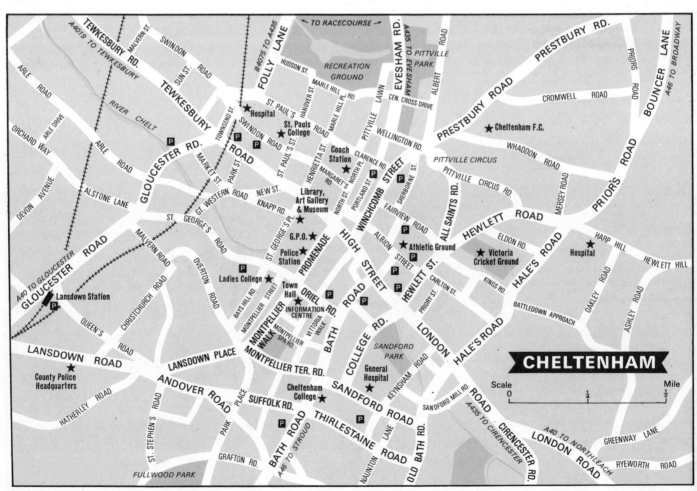

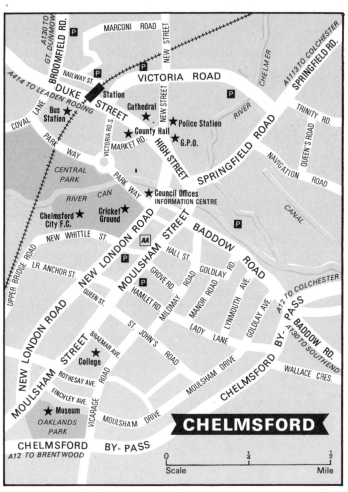

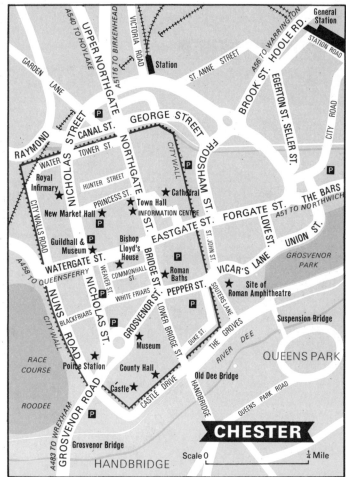

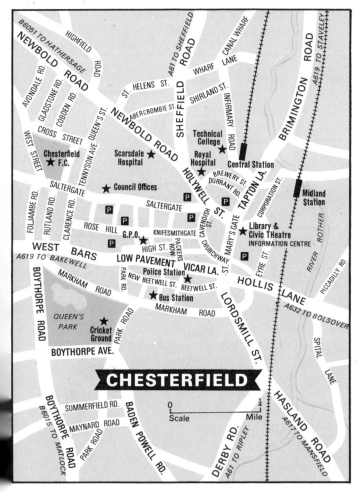

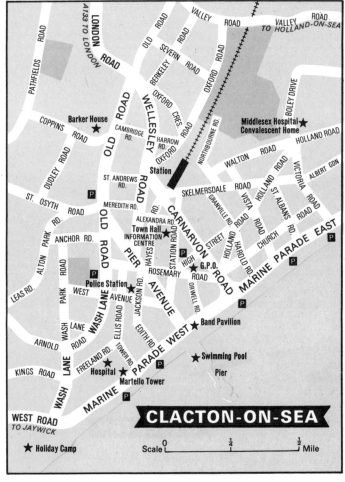

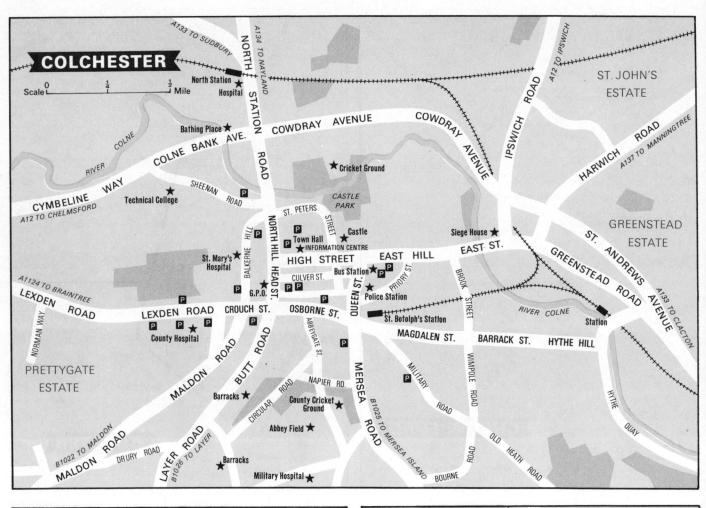

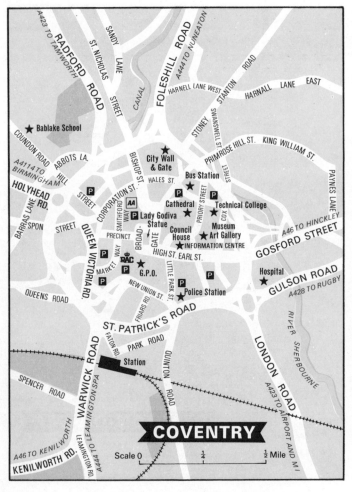

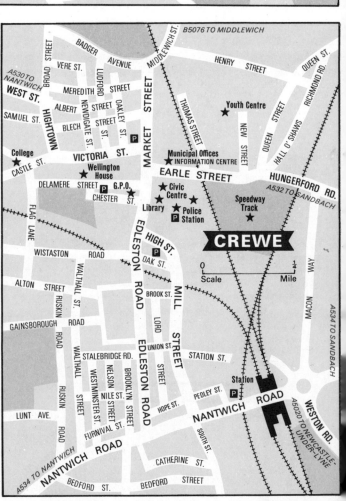

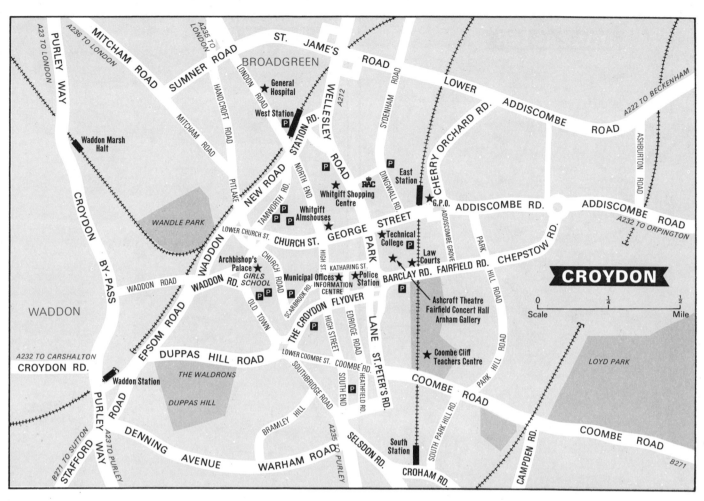

CROYDON

PURLEY WAY · A23 TO LONDON · A236 TO LONDON · MITCHAM ROAD · SUMNER ROAD · A235 TO LONDON · ST. JAMES'S ROAD · BROADGREEN · WELLESLEY ROAD · A212 · LOWER · ADDISCOMBE · ROAD · A222 TO BECKENHAM · ASHBURTON ROAD · CHERRY ORCHARD RD. · ADDISCOMBE ROAD · General Hospital · West Station · HANDCROFT ROAD · LONDON ROAD · MITCHAM ROAD · PITLAKE · NEW ROAD · NORTH END · STATION RD. · TAMWORTH RD. · East Station · SYDENHAM ROAD · DINGWALL RD. · RAC · G.P.O. · ADDISCOMBE RD. · ADDISCOMBE ROAD · A232 TO ORPINGTON · Waddon Marsh Halt · CROYDON · BY-PASS · WANDLE PARK · WADDON · WADDON ROAD · LOWER CHURCH ST. · Whitgift Shopping Centre · Whitgift Almshouses · CHURCH ST. · GEORGE STREET · Technical College · ADDISCOMBE GROVE · PARK · HIGH ST. · KATHARING ST. · Law Courts · FAIRFIELD RD. · CHEPSTOW RD. · WADDON · WADDON RD. · Archbishop's Palace · GIRLS SCHOOL · CHURCH ROAD · Municipal Offices · INFORMATION CENTRE · Police Station · BARCLAY RD. · FAIRFIELD RD. · HILL ROAD · WADDON · SCARBROOK RD. · THE CROYDON FLYOVER · OLD TOWN · EPSOM ROAD · DUPPAS HILL ROAD · Ashcroft Theatre Fairfield Concert Hall Arnham Gallery · PARK HILL ROAD · LOYD PARK · Scale · 0 · ¼ · ½ · Mile · WADDON · A232 TO CARSHALTON · CROYDON RD. · THE WALDRONS · Waddon Station · DUPPAS HILL · LOWER COOMBE ST. · HIGH STREET · EDRIDGE ROAD · COOMBE RD. · LANE · ST. PETER'S RD. · Coombe Cliff Teachers Centre · COOMBE ROAD · COOMBE ROAD · B271 TO SUTTON · PURLEY ROAD · A23 TO PURLEY · STAFFORD WAY · DENNING AVENUE · BRAMLEY HILL · SOUTHBRIDGE ROAD · SOUTH END · HEATHFIELD RD. · WARHAM ROAD · A235 TO PURLEY · SELSDON RD. · South Station · SOUTH PARK HILL RD. · CAMPDEN RD. · CROHAM RD. · B271

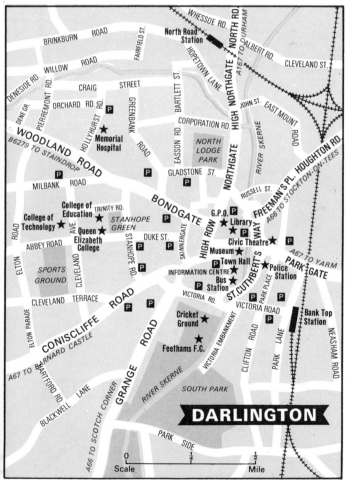

DARLINGTON

BRINKBURN ROAD · WHESSOE RD. · North Road Station · NORTH RD. · A167 TO DURHAM · ALBERT RD. · CLEVELAND ST. · WILLOW ROAD · FAIRFIELD ST. · HOPETOWN LANE · DENESIDE RD. · CRAIG STREET · ORCHARD RD. · GREENBANK · BARTLETT ST. · CORPORATION RD. · EASSON RD. · JOHN ST. · EAST MOUNT ROAD · WOODLAND ROAD · B6279 TO STAINDROP · PIERREMONT RD. · HOLLYHURST RD. · Memorial Hospital · ROAD · NORTH LODGE PARK · RIVER SKERNE · DENE GR. · GLADSTONE ST. · NORTHGATE · HIGH NORTHGATE · HOUGHTON RD. · A66 TO STOCKTON-ON-TEES · MILBANK ROAD · RUSSELL ST. · FREEMAN'S PL. · College of Technology · College of Education · TRINITY RD. · STANHOPE GREEN · Queen Elizabeth College · BONDGATE · G.P.O. · Library · HIGH ROW · FREEMAN'S WAY · ABBEY ROAD · AVE. · DUKE ST. · STANHOPE RD. · SKINNERGATE · Civic Theatre · A67 TO YARM · ELTON · ROAD · SPORTS GROUND · CLEVELAND · Museum · Town Hall · INFORMATION CENTRE · Bus Station · ST. CUTHBERT'S WAY · PARK PLACE · Police Station · PARKGATE · ELTON PARADE · CLEVELAND TERRACE · VICTORIA RD. · VICTORIA ROAD · CONISCLIFFE ROAD · GRANGE ROAD · Cricket Ground · CLIFTON ROAD · PARK LANE · VICTORIA EMBANKMENT · Bank Top Station · A67 TO SCOTCH CORNER · BARNARD CASTLE · HARTFORD RD. · Feethams F.C. · RIVER SKERNE · SOUTH PARK · NEASHAM ROAD · BLACKWELL LANE · A66 TO SCOTCH CORNER · PARK SIDE · Scale · 0 · ½ · Mile

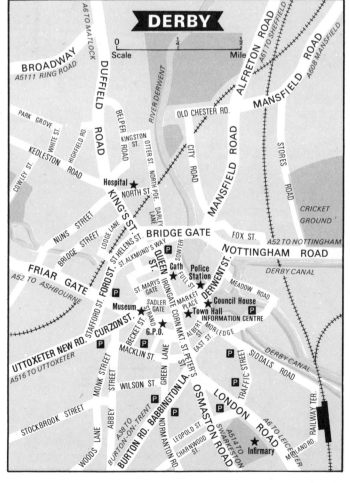

DERBY

A610 TO MATLOCK · BROADWAY · A5111 RING ROAD · ALFRETON ROAD · SHEFFIELD · MANSFIELD ROAD · A608 MANSFIELD · Scale · 0 · ½ · Mile · A61 TO SHEFFIELD · DUFFIELD ROAD · RIVER DERWENT · OLD CHESTER RD. · PARK GROVE · WHITE ST. · BELPER ROAD · KINGSTON ST. · OTTER ST. · CITY ROAD · STORES ROAD · KEDLESTON ROAD · COWLEY ST. · HIGHFIELD RD. · NORTH PDE. · DARLEY LANE · CRICKET GROUND · KING'S ST. · Hospital · NORTH ST. · NUNS STREET · LODGE LANE · BRIDGE GATE · FOX ST. · A52 TO NOTTINGHAM · NOTTINGHAM ROAD · DERBY CANAL · BRIDGE STREET · ST. HELENS ST. · ST. ALKMUND'S WAY · FRIAR GATE · A52 TO ASHBOURNE · FORD ST. · ST. MARYS GATE · SOWTER · Cath · Police Station · MEADOW ROAD · QUEEN ST. · IRONGATE · CORN MKT · Council House · Town Hall · INFORMATION CENTRE · MARKET PLACE · DERWENT ST. · UTTOXETER NEW RD. · A516 TO UTTOXETER · STAFFORD ST. · CURZON ST. · BECKET LANE · SADLER GATE · Museum · ALBERT ST. · ST. PETER'S ST. · EAST ST. · MORLEDGE · DERBY CANAL · G.P.O. · MACKLIN ST. · GREEN LANE · MONK STREET · WILSON STREET · ABBEY STREET · SIDDALS ROAD · TRAFFIC STREET · LONDON ROAD · A6 TO LEICESTER · STOCKBROOK STREET · WOODS LANE · A38 TO BURTON-ON-TRENT · BURTON RD. · NORMANTON RD. · BABBINGTON LA. · ST. PETER'S ST. · LEOPOLD ST. · CHARNWOOD ST. · OSMASTON ROAD · A514 TO SWARKESTONE · Infirmary · RAILWAY TER. · MIDLAND RD.

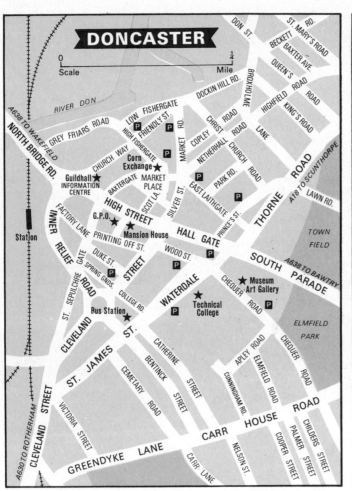

DONCASTER

0 Scale ¼ Mile

RIVER DON
A638 TO WAKEFIELD
NORTH BRIDGE RD.
Station
INNER RELIEF ROAD
A630 TO ROTHERHAM
CLEVELAND STREET
VICTORIA STREET
ST. SEPULCHRE GATE
Factory Lane
Duke St.
Spring Gnds.
College Rd.
GREY FRIARS ROAD
CHURCH WAY
Corn Exchange ★
Guildhall ★
INFORMATION CENTRE
Baxtergate
G.P.O. ■
Printing Off St.
Mansion House ★
HIGH STREET
Scot La.
Cleveland St.
ST. JAMES ST.
CEMETARY ROAD
CATHERINE STREET
BENTINCK STREET
CUNNINGHAM RD.
GREENDYKE LANE
LOW FISHERGATE
HIGH FISHERGATE
Friendly St.
MARKET RD.
COPLEY ROAD
CHRIST CHURCH ROAD
NETHERHALL ROAD
Silver St.
Park Rd.
East Laithgate
Prince's St.
WOOD ST.
Chequer Road
WATERDALE
Technical College ★
Bus Station ★
APLEY ROAD
ELMFIELD ROAD
CHEQUER ROAD
MARKET PLACE
HALL GATE
SOUTH PARADE
CARR HOUSE ROAD
CARR LANE
NELSON ST.
COOPER STREET
PALMER STREET
CHILDERS STREET
DOCKIN HILL RD.
HIGHFIELD ROAD
KING'S ROAD
BROXHOLME LANE
QUEEN'S ROAD
DON ST.
ST. MARY'S ROAD
BECKETT AVE.
BAXTER AVE.
THORNE ROAD
LAWN RD.
A18 TO SCUNTHORPE
A638 TO BAWTRY
TOWN FIELD
ELMFIELD PARK
Museum Art Gallery ★

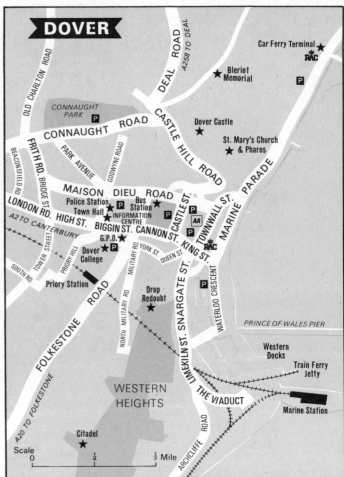

DOVER

0 Scale ¼ ½ Mile

OLD CHARLTON ROAD
CONNAUGHT ROAD
CONNAUGHT PARK
DEAL ROAD
A258 TO DEAL
Car Ferry Terminal ★ RAC
Bleriot Memorial ★
CASTLE HILL ROAD
Dover Castle ★
St. Mary's Church ★ & Pharos
FRITH RD.
BRIDGE ST.
PARK AVENUE
GODWYNE ROAD
MAISON DIEU ROAD
BEACONSFIELD RD.
LONDON RD.
A2 TO CANTERBURY
HIGH ST.
Police Station ★
Town Hall ★
Bus Station ★
INFORMATION CENTRE
BIGGIN ST.
CANNON ST.
G.P.O. ■
Dover College ★
Priory Station
Priory Hill
TOWER STREET
SOUTH RD.
NORTH MILITARY RD.
MILITARY RD.
YORK ST.
QUEEN ST.
LIMEKILN ST.
SNARGATE ST.
KING ST.
CASTLE ST.
TOWNWALL ST.
AA
RAC
WATERLOO CRESCENT
MARINE PARADE
Drop Redoubt ★
THE VIADUCT
ARCHCLIFFE ROAD
WESTERN HEIGHTS
Citadel ★
A20 TO FOLKESTONE
FOLKESTONE ROAD
A20 TO FOLKESTONE
PRINCE OF WALES PIER
Western Docks
Train Ferry Jetty
Marine Station

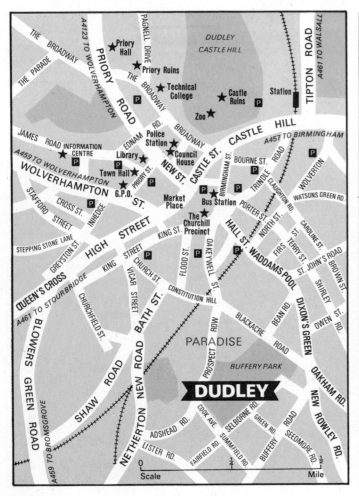

DUDLEY

0 Scale ¼ Mile

THE BROADWAY
A4123 TO WOLVERHAMPTON
THE PARADE
PAGNELL DRIVE
Priory Hall ★
Priory Ruins ★
Technical College ★
THE BROADWAY
PRIORY ROAD
DUDLEY CASTLE HILL
Castle Ruins ★
Zoo ★
Station
TIPTON ROAD
A461 TO WALSALL
JAMES ROAD
A459 TO WOLVERHAMPTON
INFORMATION CENTRE ★
Library ★
Ednam Rd.
Police Station ★
Council House ★
CASTLE ST.
CASTLE HILL
A457 TO BIRMINGHAM
Town Hall ★
Priory St.
G.P.O. ■
NEW ST.
BROADWAY
BIRMINGHAM ST.
BOURNE ST.
TRINDLE ROAD
CLAUGHTON RD.
WOLVERTON
WATSONS GREEN RD.
WOLVERHAMPTON
STAFFORD STREET
CROSS ST.
INHEDGE
Market Place
Bus Station ★
HALL ST.
WADDAMS POOL
PORTER ST.
NORTH ST.
FIRS ST.
CAROLINE ST.
ST. JOHN'S ROAD
TERRY ST.
BROWN ST.
SHIRLEY ROAD
QUEEN'S CROSS
A461 TO STOURBRIDGE
STEPPING STONE LANE
GREYSTON ST.
The Churchill Precinct ★
HIGH STREET
KING STREET
CHURCH ST.
VICAR STREET
FLOOD ST.
OAKEYWELL ST.
CONSTITUTION HILL
BLACKACRE ROAD
BEAN RD.
DIXON'S GREEN
OWEN ST.
BLOWERS GREEN ROAD
CHURCHFIELD ST.
BATH ST.
NEW ROAD
SHAW ROAD
PARADISE
BUFFERY PARK
PROSPECT ROW
A459 TO BROMSGROVE
NETHERTON
COOK AVE.
LISTER RD.
ADSHEAD RD.
FAIRFIELD RD.
SUMMFIELD RD.
SELBORNE RD.
GREEN RD.
BUFFERY ROAD
SEEDMORE RD.
NEW ROWLEY RD.
OAKHAM RD.

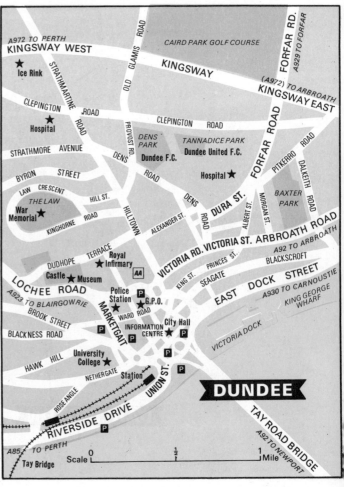

DUNDEE

0 Scale ¼ ½ 1 Mile

A972 TO PERTH
KINGSWAY WEST
GLAMIS ROAD
OLD GLAMIS ROAD
CAIRD PARK GOLF COURSE
KINGSWAY
FORFAR RD.
A929 TO FORFAR
(A972) TO ARBROATH
KINGSWAY EAST
Ice Rink ★
STRATHMARTINE
CLEPINGTON ROAD
CLEPINGTON ROAD
Hospital ★
STRATHMORE AVENUE
PROVOST RD.
DENS RD.
DENS PARK
TANNADICE PARK
Dundee United F.C. ★
Dundee F.C. ★
FORFAR ROAD
PITKERRO ROAD
DALKEITH ROAD
BYRON STREET
DENS ROAD
Hospital ★
DURA ST.
BAXTER PARK
MORGAN ST.
ALBERT ST.
LAW CRESCENT
THE LAW
HILL ST.
ALEXANDER ST.
War Memorial ★
KINGHORNE ROAD
HILLTOWN
VICTORIA RD.
VICTORIA ST.
ARBROATH ROAD
A92 TO ARBROATH
DUDHOPE TERRACE
Royal Infirmary ★
Castle ★
Museum ★
AA
KING ST.
PRINCES ST.
SEAGATE
BLACKSCROFT
EAST DOCK STREET
A930 TO CARNOUSTIE
KING GEORGE WHARF
LOCHEE ROAD
A923 TO BLAIRGOWRIE
Police Station ★
G.P.O. ■
WARD ROAD
MARKETGAIT
INFORMATION CENTRE ★
City Hall ★
BROOK STREET
BLACKNESS ROAD
VICTORIA DOCK
HAWK HILL
University College ★
NETHERGATE
Station
UNION ST.
RIVERSIDE DRIVE
A85 TO PERTH
Tay Bridge
ROSE ANGLE
TAY ROAD BRIDGE
A92 TO NEWPORT

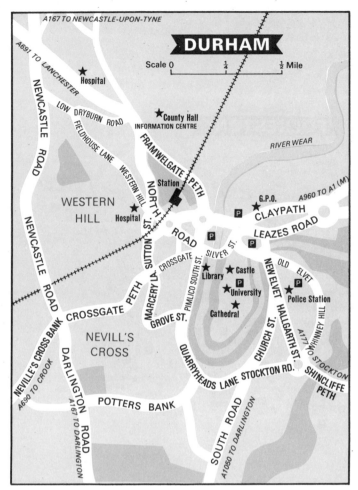

DURHAM

A167 TO NEWCASTLE-UPON-TYNE

Scale 0 ¼ ½ Mile

A691 TO LANCHESTER

★ Hospital

★ County Hall
INFORMATION CENTRE

RIVER WEAR

NEWCASTLE ROAD

LOW DRYBURN ROAD

FIELDHOUSE LANE

WESTERN HILL

FRAMWELGATE PETH

Station

WESTERN HILL

★ Hospital

NORTH ROAD

SILVER ST.

G.P.O.

A960 TO A1 (M)

LEAZES ROAD

★ CLAYPATH

P

P

NEVILLE'S CROSS BANK

CROSSGATE PETH

MARCERY LA.

SUTTON ST.

PIMLICO SOUTH ST.

CROSSGATE

GROVE ST.

★ Library
★ Castle
★ University
★ Cathedral

NEW ELVET

OLD ELVET

★ Police Station

HALLGARTH ST.

CHURCH ST.

A177 TO STOCKTON

WHINNEY HILL

SHINCLIFFE PETH

NEVILL'S CROSS

A690 TO CROOK

DARLINGTON ROAD

A167 TO DARLINGTON

POTTERS BANK

QUARRYHEADS LANE

STOCKTON RD.

SOUTH ROAD

A1050 TO DARLINGTON

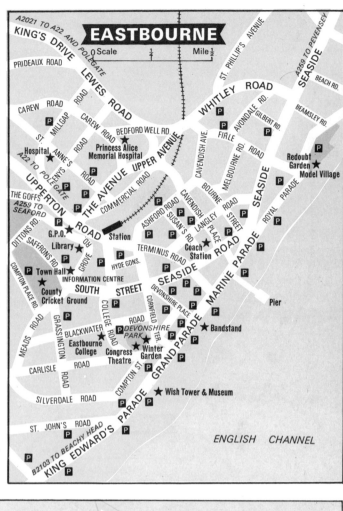

EASTBOURNE

A2021 TO A22 AND POLEGATE

Scale 0 ¼ ½ Mile

KING'S DRIVE

LEWES ROAD

A259 TO PEVENSEY

ST. PHILLIP'S AVENUE

PRIDEAUX ROAD

WHITLEY ROAD

SEASIDE

BEACH RD.

CAREW ROAD

MILLGAP

CAREW ROAD

BEDFORD WELL RD.

AVONDALE RD.

GILBERT RD.

BEAMSLEY RD.

ST. ANNE'S

ST. JOHN'S

★ Princess Alice Memorial Hospital

FIRLE

CAVENDISH AVE.

MELBOURNE RD.

★ Hospital

UPPERTON ROAD

THE AVENUE

UPPER AVENUE

A22 TO POLEGATE

ASHFORD ROAD

CAVENDISH

LANGLEY ROAD

SEASIDE

ROYAL PARADE

Redoubt Garden ★
Model Village

THE GOFFS

A259 TO SEAFORD

COMMERCIAL ROAD

BOURNE ST.

SUSAN'S RD.

PLACE

DITTONS RD.

G.P.O.

Station

TERMINUS ROAD

Coach Station

MARINE PARADE

SAFFRONS RD.

★ Library

GROVE

HYDE GDNS.

SEASIDE ROAD

COMPTON PLACE RD.

★ Town Hall
INFORMATION CENTRE

SOUTH STREET

DEVONSHIRE PLACE

Pier

County Cricket Ground

COLLEGE ROAD

CORNFIELD ROAD

GRAND PARADE

★ Bandstand

MEADS ROAD

GRASSINGTON

BLACKWATER ROAD

DEVONSHIRE PARK

Eastbourne College

Congress Theatre

Winter Garden

CARLISLE ROAD

COMPTON PLACE RD.

★ Wish Tower & Museum

SILVERDALE ROAD

KING EDWARD'S PARADE

ST. JOHN'S ROAD

B2103 TO BEACHY HEAD

ENGLISH CHANNEL

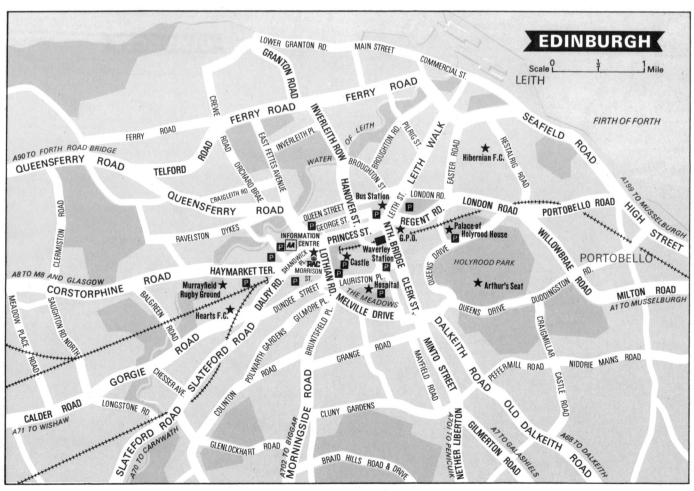

EDINBURGH

LOWER GRANTON RD.

MAIN STREET

COMMERCIAL ST.

LEITH

Scale 0 ½ 1 Mile

GRANTON ROAD

FERRY ROAD

SEAFIELD ROAD

FIRTH OF FORTH

CREWE ROAD

FERRY ROAD

FERRY ROAD

INVERLEITH ROW

EAST FETTES AVENUE

INVERLEITH PL.

WATER OF LEITH

BROUGHTON RD.

PILRIG ST.

LEITH WALK

EASTER ROAD

RESTALRIG ROAD

A199 TO MUSSELBURGH

A90 TO FORTH ROAD BRIDGE

★ Hibernian F.C.

QUEENSFERRY ROAD

TELFORD

ORCHARD BRAE

CRAIGLEITH RD.

QUEENSFERRY ROAD

BROUGHTON ST.

LEITH ST.

LONDON RD.

LONDON ROAD

PORTOBELLO ROAD

HIGH STREET

HANOVER ST.

Bus Station

RAVELSTON

DYKES

QUEEN STREET

GEORGE ST.

REGENT RD.

Palace of ★ Holyrood House

G.P.O.

WILLOWBRAE ROAD

PORTOBELLO

CLERMISTON ROAD

INFORMATION CENTRE

AA

PRINCES ST.

NTH. BRIDGE

A8 TO M8 AND GLASGOW

HAYMARKET TER.

SHANDWICK PL.

RAC

MORRISON ST.

Waverley Station

★ Castle

HOLYROOD PARK

CORSTORPHINE ROAD

Murrayfield ★ Rugby Ground

DALRY RD.

LOTHIAN RD.

LAURISTON PL.

★ Hospital

QUEENS DRIVE

★ Arthur's Seat

MILTON ROAD
A1 TO MUSSELBURGH

MEADOW PLACE

SAUGHTON RD. NORTH

BALGREEN

DUNDEE STREET

GILMORE PL.

THE MEADOWS

MELVILLE DRIVE

QUEENS DRIVE

DUDDINGSTON

CRAIGMILLAR

Hearts F.C. ★

GORGIE

CHESSER AVE.

SLATEFORD ROAD

POLWARTH GARDENS

BRUNTSFIELD PL.

GRANGE ROAD

MINTO STREET

MAYFIELD ROAD

DALKEITH ROAD

PEFFERMILL ROAD

CASTLE ROAD

NIDDRIE MAINS ROAD

CALDER ROAD

A71 TO WISHAW

LONGSTONE RD.

COLINTON

MORNINGSIDE ROAD

CLUNY GARDENS

OLD DALKEITH ROAD

A68 TO DALKEITH

GLENLOCKHART ROAD

A702 TO BIGGAR

BRAID HILLS ROAD & DRIVE

GILMERTON ROAD

NETHER LIBERTON

A701 TO PENICUIK

A772 TO GALASHIELS

A70 TO CARNWATH

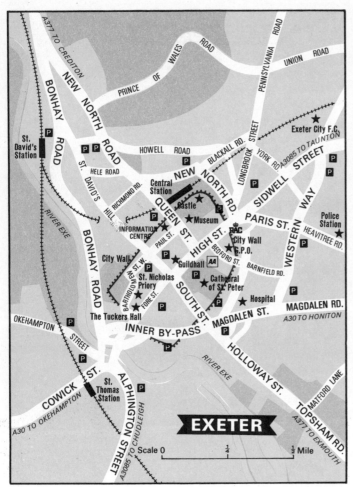

EXETER

A377 TO CREDITON
NEW NORTH ROAD
PRINCE OF WALES ROAD
UNION ROAD
PENNSYLVANIA ROAD
BONHAY ROAD
St. David's Station
HOWELL ROAD
ST. DAVID'S HILL
HELE ROAD
RICHMOND RD.
BLACKALL RD.
LONGBROOK ST.
YORK RD. A3085 TO TAUNTON
Exeter City F.C.
Central Station
Castle
Museum
INFORMATION CENTRE
QUEEN ST.
PAUL ST.
City Wall
BARTHOLOMEW ST. W.
St. Nicholas Priory
FORE ST.
The Tuckers Hall
Guildhall
AA
St. James' ST.
City Wall
High ST.
BEDFORD ST.
B.P.O.
Cathedral of St. Peter
Hospital
PARIS ST.
SIDWELL STREET
WESTERN WAY
HEAVITREE RD.
Police Station
BARNFIELD RD.
MAGDALEN RD.
MAGDALEN ST.
A30 TO HONITON
SOUTH ST.
INNER BY-PASS
BONHAY ROAD
RIVER EXE
OKEHAMPTON STREET
COWICK ST.
A30 TO OKEHAMPTON
St. Thomas Station
ALPHINGTON STREET
A3085 TO CHUDLEIGH
HOLLOWAY ST.
RIVER EXE
MATFORD LANE
TOPSHAM RD.
A377 TO EXMOUTH
Scale 0   ¼   ½ Mile

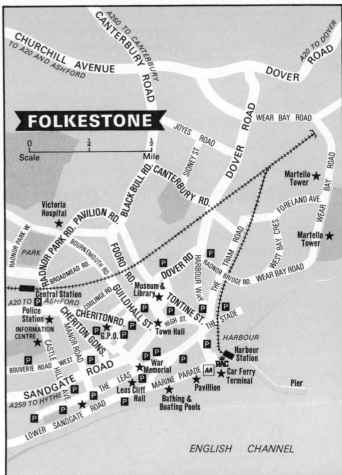

FOLKESTONE

A260 TO CANTERBURY
CANTERBURY ROAD
CHURCHILL AVENUE
TO A20 AND ASHFORD
A20 TO DOVER
DOVER ROAD
Scale 0   ¼   ½ Mile
JOYES ROAD
WEAR BAY ROAD
BLACK BULL RD. CANTERBURY RD.
SIDNEY ST.
DOVER ROAD
Martello Tower
RADNOR PARK RD. PAVILION RD.
Victoria Hospital
RADNOR PARK W.
BROADMEAD RD.
BOURNEMOUTH RD.
FOORD RD.
DOVER RD.
HARBOUR WAY
RADNOR BRIDGE RD.
THE TRAM ROAD
FORELAND AVE.
WEST BAY CRES.
WEAR BAY ROAD
Martello Tower
Central Station
A20 TO ASHFORD
COOLINGE RD.
GUILDHALL ST.
Museum & Library
TONTINE ST.
THE STADE
HARBOUR
Police Station
CHERITON RD.
CHERITON GDNS.
MANOR ROAD
G.P.O.
HIGH ST.
Town Hall
Harbour Station
INFORMATION CENTRE
CASTLE HILL AVE.
WEST
BOUVERIE ROAD
War Memorial
AA
RAC
Car Ferry Terminal
SANDGATE ROAD
A259 TO HYTHE
THE LEAS
MARINE PARADE
Pavillion
Pier
Leas Cliff Hall
Bathing & Boating Pools
SANDGATE ROAD
LOWER SANDGATE ROAD

ENGLISH CHANNEL

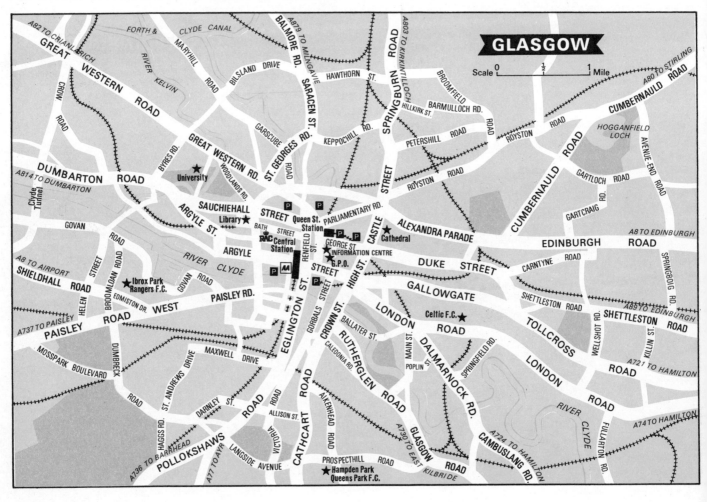

GLASGOW

A82 TO CRIANLARICH
FORTH & CLYDE CANAL
GREAT WESTERN ROAD
BALMORE RD.
A879 TO MILNGAVIE
A803 TO KIRKINTILLOCH
SPRINGBURN ROAD
A80 TO STIRLING
Scale 0   ½   1 Mile
CUMBERNAULD ROAD
RIVER KELVIN
MARYHILL ROAD
CROW ROAD
BILSLAND DRIVE
HAWTHORN ST.
SARACEN ST.
BROOMFIELD RD.
BARMULLOCH RD.
HILLKIRK ST.
PETERSHILL ROAD
ROYSTON ROAD
HOGGANFIELD LOCH
DUMBARTON ROAD
A814 TO DUMBARTON
GREAT WESTERN RD.
BYRES RD.
University
WOODLANDS RD.
ST. GEORGES RD.
GARSCUBE ROAD
KEPPOCHILL RD.
ROYSTON ROAD
GARTLOCH ROAD
AVENUE-END ROAD
CUMBERNAULD ROAD
Clyde Tunnel
SAUCHIEHALL STREET
ARGYLE ST.
Library
BATH STREET
Queen St. Station
PARLIAMENTARY RD.
CASTLE STREET
Cathedral
ALEXANDRA PARADE
GARTCRAIG RD.
EDINBURGH ROAD
A8 TO EDINBURGH
GOVAN ROAD
RAC
Central Station
RENFIELD ST.
George St.
INFORMATION CENTRE
G.P.O.
HIGH ST.
DUKE STREET
CARNTYNE ROAD
SPRINGBOIG RD.
A8 TO AIRPORT
SHIELDHALL ROAD
ARGYLE RIVER CLYDE
AA
Ibrox Park Rangers F.C.
BROOMLOAN ROAD
EDMISTON DR.
GOVAN ROAD
PAISLEY RD.
GALLOWGATE
SHETTLESTON ROAD
WELLSHOT RD.
A89 TO EDINBURGH
SHETTLESTON ROAD
HELEN STREET
PAISLEY ROAD WEST
Celtic F.C.
LONDON ROAD
TOLLCROSS ROAD
A737 TO PAISLEY
PAISLEY ROAD
MOSSPARK BOULEVARD
DUMBRECK ROAD
EGLINTON ST.
MAXWELL DRIVE
GORBALS STREET
CROWN ST.
BALLATER ST.
RUTHERGLEN ROAD
MAIN ST.
LONDON ROAD
CALEDONIA RD.
DALMARNOCK RD.
SPRINGFIELD RD.
LONDON ROAD
RIVER CLYDE
FULLARTON RD.
ST. ANDREWS DRIVE
DARNLEY ST.
ALLISON ST.
AIKENHEAD ROAD
POPLIN ST.
A724 TO HAMILTON
CAMBUSLANG RD.
A74 TO HAMILTON
POLLOKSHAWS
HAGGS RD.
A736 TO BARRHEAD
LANGSIDE AVENUE
VICTORIA ROAD
CATHCART ROAD
A77 TO AYR
PROSPECTHILL ROAD
Hampden Park Queens Park F.C.
GLASGOW ROAD
A730 TO EAST KILBRIDE
A721 TO HAMILTON

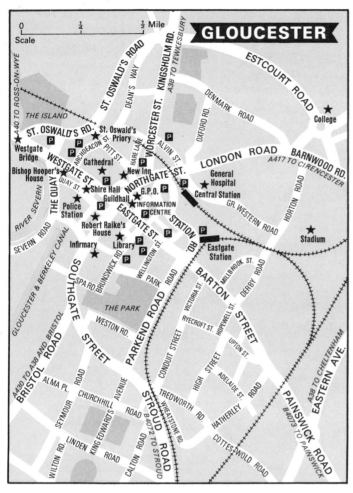

GLOUCESTER

Scale 0 ¼ ½ Mile

A40 TO ROSS-ON-WYE
ST. OSWALD'S ROAD
KINGSHOLM RD.
DEAN'S WAY
WORCESTER ST.
ESTCOURT ROAD
DENMARK ROAD
OXFORD RD.
ALVIN ST.
★ College
THE ISLAND
ST. OSWALD'S RD.
★ St. Oswald's Priory
ARCHDEACON ST.
PITT ST.
HARE LANE
Westgate Bridge
WESTGATE ST.
Bishop Hooper's House
Cathedral ★
New Inn
NORTHGATE ST.
LONDON ROAD
BARNWOOD RD.
A417 TO CIRENCESTER
General Hospital ★
A38 TO TEWKESBURY
Shire Hall
Guildhall
G.P.O.
QUAY ST.
Police Station
EASTGATE ST.
INFORMATION CENTRE
Central Station
HORTON ROAD
Robert Raike's House
STATION RD.
GR. WESTERN ROAD
THE QUAY
RIVER SEVERN
SEVERN ROAD
Infirmary
Library
Eastgate Station
Stadium ★
GLOUCESTER & BERKELEY CANAL
SPA RD.
BRUNSWICK RD.
WELLINGTON ST.
PARK ROAD
MILLBROOK ST.
DERBY ROAD
SOUTHGATE STREET
THE PARK
WESTON RD.
PARKEND ROAD
RYECROFT ST.
HOPEWELL ST.
UPTON ST.
BARTON STREET
VICTORIA ST.
HIGH STREET
ADELAIDE ST.
A38 TO CHELTENHAM
EASTERN AVE.
BRISTOL ROAD
A430 TO A38 AND BRISTOL
ALMA PL.
SEYMOUR
CHURCHHILL
KING EDWARDS AVENUE
CONDUIT STREET
TREDWORTH RD.
HATHERLEY
WHEATSTONE RD.
B4072 TO STROUD
STROUD ROAD
WILTON RD.
LINDEN ROAD
CALTON ROAD
COTTESWOLD ROAD
PAINSWICK ROAD
B4073 TO PAINSWICK

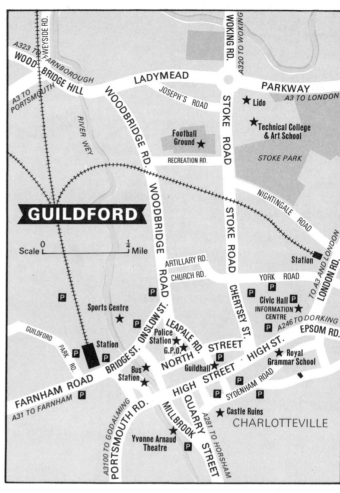

GUILDFORD

Scale 0 ¼ Mile

WOODBRIDGE HILL
WEYSIDE RD.
A323 TO FARNBOROUGH
WOKING RD.
A320 TO WOKING
A3 TO PORTSMOUTH
LADYMEAD
JOSEPH'S ROAD
PARKWAY
A3 TO LONDON
★ Lido
RIVER WEY
WOODBRIDGE RD.
STOKE ROAD
★ Technical College & Art School
Football Ground ★
RECREATION RD.
STOKE PARK
NIGHTINGALE ROAD
ARTILLERY RD.
CHURCH RD.
CHERTSEY ST.
YORK ROAD
Station
TO A3 AND LONDON
LONDON RD.
Sports Centre ★
ONSLOW ST.
LEAPALE RD.
Civic Hall
INFORMATION CENTRE
A246 TO DORKING
EPSOM RD.
Station
BRIDGE ST.
Police Station
G.P.O.
NORTH STREET
Guildhall
HIGH STREET
HIGH ST.
★ Royal Grammar School
PARK RD.
Bus Station ★
QUARRY
SYDENHAM ROAD
FARNHAM ROAD
A31 TO FARNHAM
A3100 TO GODALMING
PORTSMOUTH RD.
MILLBROOK
★ Castle Ruins
CHARLOTTEVILLE
A281 TO HORSHAM
Yvonne Arnaud Theatre
MILLBROOK STREET

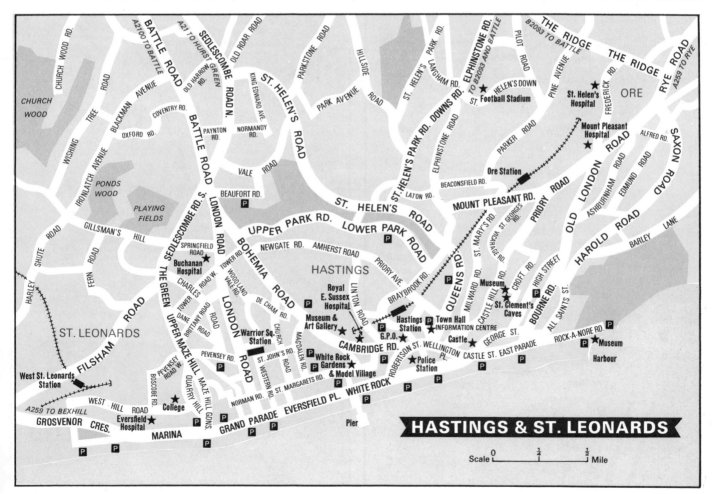

HASTINGS & ST. LEONARDS

Scale 0 ¼ ½ Mile

CHURCH WOOD RD.
BATTLE ROAD
A2100 TO BATTLE
SEDLESCOMBE ROAD N.
A21 TO HURST GREEN
OLD HARROW ROAD
OLD ROAR ROAD
PARKSTONE ROAD
HILLSIDE
ST. HELEN'S PARK RD.
LANGHAM RD.
ELPHINSTONE RD.
TO B2093 AND BATTLE
PILOT ROAD
B2093 TO BATTLE
THE RIDGE
THE RIDGE
RYE ROAD
A259 TO RYE
CHURCH WOOD
TREE ROAD
BLACKMAN AVENUE
COVENTRY RD.
KING EDWARD AVE.
ST. HELEN'S ROAD
PARK AVENUE
ST. HELEN'S DOWN
PINE AVENUE
St. Helen's Hospital ★
ORE
FREDERICK RD.
WISHING TREE ROAD
OXFORD RD.
PAYNTON RD.
NORMANDY RD.
PARK AVENUE ROAD
★ Football Stadium
Mount Pleasant Hospital ★
ALFRED RD.
SAXON ROAD
IRONLATCH AVENUE
PONDS WOOD
BATTLE ROAD
VALE ROAD
ELPHINSTONE ROAD
PARKER ROAD
Ore Station
OLD LONDON ROAD
ASHBURNHAM ROAD
EDMUND ROAD
PLAYING FIELDS
GILLSMAN'S HILL
SEDLESCOMBE RD. S.
LONDON ROAD
BEAUFORT RD.
ST. HELEN'S ROAD
BEACONSFIELD RD.
LATON RD.
MOUNT PLEASANT RD.
BARLEY LANE
SHUTE ROAD
FERN ROAD
THE GREEN
CHARLES ROAD
Springfield Road
Buchanan Hospital
TOWER ROAD W.
UPPER PARK RD.
LOWER PARK ROAD
NEWGATE RD.
AMHERST ROAD
HASTINGS
PRIORY AVE.
ST. MARY'S RD.
QUEENS RD.
ST. GEORGE'S RD.
MILWARD RD.
Museum ★
CASTLE HILL
CROFT RD.
HIGH STREET
HAROLD ROAD
BOURNE RD.
HARLEY SHUTE ROAD
TOWER ROAD
BRITTANY ROAD
DANE ROAD
BOHEMIA ROAD
DE CHAM RD.
WOODLAND VALE RD.
Royal E. Sussex Hospital ★
LINTON ROAD
BRAYBROOK RD.
ST. Clement's Caves ★
ST. LEONARDS
UPPER MAZE HILL
Warrior Sq. Station
CHURCH ROAD
Museum & Art Gallery ★
Hastings Station
G.P.O.
Town Hall
INFORMATION CENTRE
Castle ★
GEORGE ST.
ALL SAINTS ST.
★ Museum
FILSHAM ROAD
PEVENSEY ROAD
ST. JOHN'S RD.
MAGDALEN RD.
White Rock Gardens & Model Village ★
CAMBRIDGE RD.
ROBERTSON ST.
WELLINGTON PL.
CASTLE ST.
EAST PARADE
ROCK-A-NORE RD.
Harbour
West St. Leonards Station
PEVENSEY ROAD W.
BOSCOBE RD.
QUARRY HILL
MAZE HILL GDNS.
WESTERN RD.
ST. MARGARETS RD.
Police Station
WHITE ROCK
WEST HILL ROAD
College ★
NORMAN RD.
GRAND PARADE
EVERSFIELD PL.
WHITE ROCK
A259 TO BEXHILL
GROSVENOR CRES.
Eversfield Hospital ★
MARINA
Pier

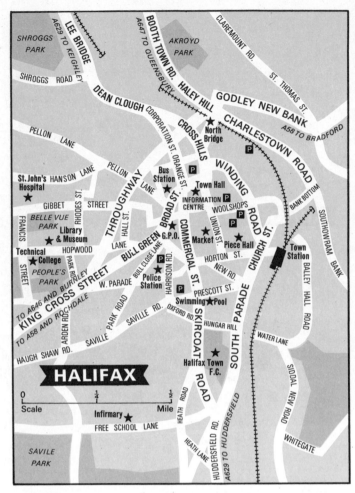

HALIFAX

Scale 0 ¼ ½ Mile

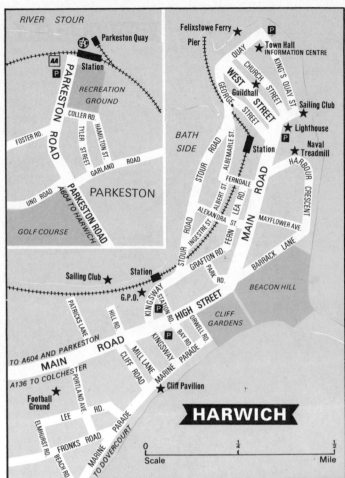

HARWICH

Scale 0 ¼ ½ Mile

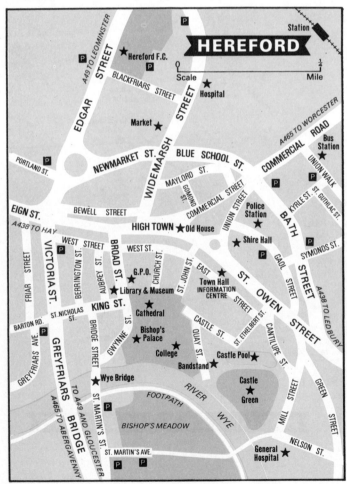

HEREFORD

Scale ¼ Mile

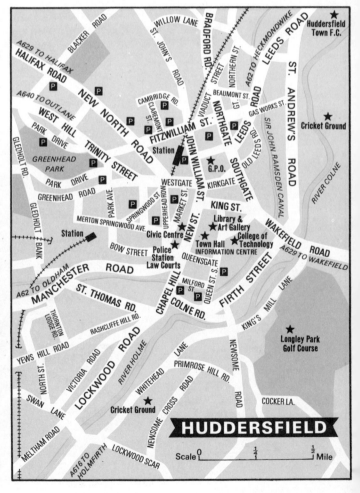

HUDDERSFIELD

Scale 0 ¼ ½ Mile

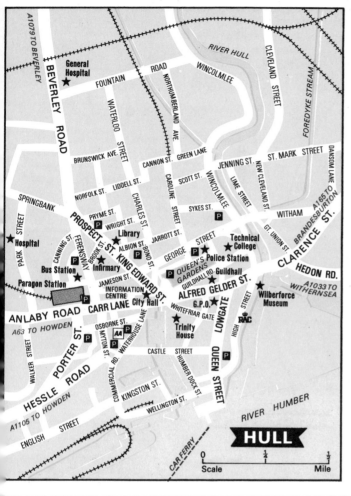

HULL

Map labels: A1079 TO BEVERLEY, General Hospital, FOUNTAIN, BEVERLEY ROAD, NORTHUMBERLAND AVE., ROAD, WINCOLMLEE, RIVER HULL, CLEVELAND STREET, FOREDYKE STREAM, WATERLOO STREET, BRUNSWICK AVE., CANNON STREET, GREEN LANE, JENNING ST., ST. MARK STREET, DANSOM LANE, BRANDESBURTON, A165 TO, NORFOLK ST., LIDDELL ST., CAROLINE, SCOTT ST., NEW CLEVELAND ST., LIME STREET, WINCOLMLEE, WITHAM, GT. UNION ST., CLARENCE ST., SPRINGBANK, PRYME ST., WRIGHT ST., CHARLES ST., ALBION ST., BOND ST., SYKES ST., JARROTT ST., GEORGE STREET, Library, Hospital, PARK STREET, FERENSWAY, ST., KING EDWARD ST., PROSPECT ST., CANNING ST., Technical College, Queen's Gardens, Police Station, HEDON RD., A1033 TO WITHERNSEA, Bus Station, Infirmary, JAMESON ST., Guildhall, Guildhall RD., ALFRED GELDER ST., Wilberforce Museum, Paragon Station, INFORMATION CENTRE, City Hall, G.P.O., WHITEFRIAR GATE, HIGH STREET, LOWGATE, RAC, ANLABY ROAD, CARR LANE, Trinity House, A63 TO HOWDEN, AA, OSBORNE ST., MYTON ST., WATERHOUSE LANE, CASTLE STREET, WALKER STREET, PORTER ST., COMMERCIAL RD., KINGSTON ST., HUMBER DOCK ST., QUEEN STREET, HESSLE ROAD, WELLINGTON STREET, A1105 TO HOWDEN, ENGLISH STREET, RIVER HUMBER, CAR FERRY, Scale, Mile

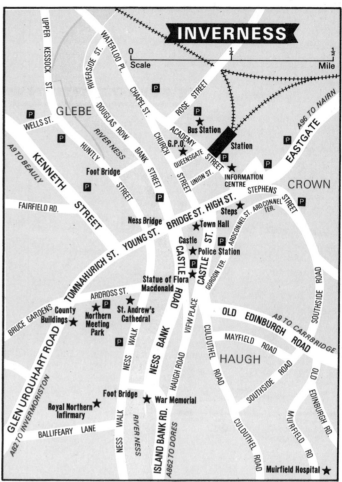

INVERNESS

Map labels: UPPER KESSOCK ST., RIVERSIDE ST., WATERLOO PL., Scale, Mile, GLEBE, WELLS ST., DOUGLAS ROW, CHAPEL ST., ROSE STREET, ACADEMY ST., Bus Station, Station, EASTGATE, A96 TO NAIRN, A9 TO BEAULY, KENNETH STREET, HUNTLY STREET, RIVER NESS, BANK STREET, CHURCH STREET, G.P.O., QUEENSGATE, UNION ST., INFORMATION CENTRE, CROWN, Foot Bridge, FAIRFIELD RD., STEPHENS STREET, Steps, Ness Bridge, BRIDGE ST., HIGH ST., Town Hall, ARDCONNEL ST., ARDCONNEL ST. TER., TOMNAHURICH ST., YOUNG ST., Castle, CASTLE ST., Police Station, CASTLE ST., GORDON TER., VIEW PLACE, OLD EDINBURGH ROAD, A9 TO CARRBRIDGE, SOUTHSIDE ROAD, Statue of Flora Macdonald, CASTLE ROAD, CULDUTHEL ROAD, GLEN URQUHART ROAD, BRUCE GARDENS, County Buildings, ARDROSS ST., Northern Meeting Park, St. Andrew's Cathedral, NESS WALK, NESS BANK, HAUGH ROAD, MAYFIELD ROAD, HAUGH, SOUTHSIDE ROAD, CULDUTHEL ROAD, MUIRFIELD RD., OLD EDINBURGH RD., A82 TO INVERMORISTON, Royal Northern Infirmary, Foot Bridge, War Memorial, NESS WALK, RIVER NESS, ISLAND BANK RD., A862 TO DORES, BALLIFEARY LANE, Muirfield Hospital

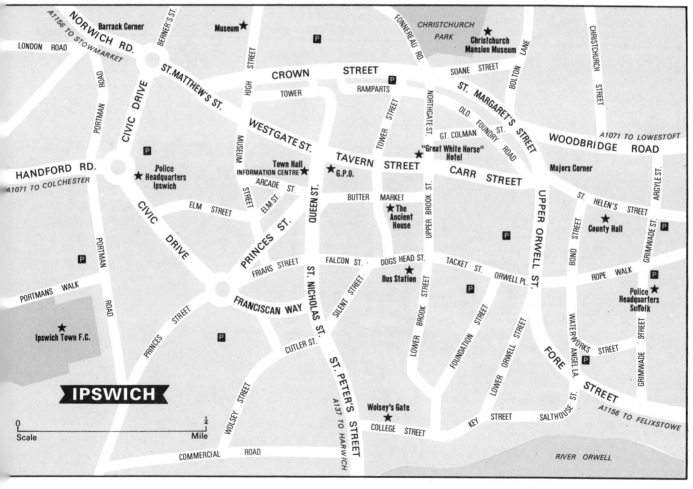

IPSWICH

Map labels: A1156 TO STOWMARKET, NORWICH RD., BARRACK CORNER, BERNER'S ST., Museum, FONNEREAU RD., CHRISTCHURCH PARK, Christchurch Mansion Museum, CHRISTCHURCH STREET, LONDON ROAD, PORTMAN ROAD, CIVIC DRIVE, ST. MATTHEW'S ST., HIGH STREET, CROWN STREET, TOWER, RAMPARTS, SOANE STREET, ST. MARGARET'S STREET, BOLTON LANE, WOODBRIDGE ROAD, A1071 TO LOWESTOFT, WESTGATE ST., TOWER STREET, NORTHGATE ST., GT. COLMAN, OLD FOUNDRY ROAD, HANDFORD RD., A1071 TO COLCHESTER, Police Headquarters Ipswich, MUSEUM STREET, Town Hall, INFORMATION CENTRE, ARCADE ST., TAVERN STREET, "Great White Horse" Hotel, CARR STREET, Majors Corner, ST. HELEN'S STREET, ARGYLE ST., CIVIC DRIVE, ELM STREET, ELM ST., QUEEN ST., G.P.O., BUTTER MARKET, UPPER BROOK ST., County Hall, BOND STREET, GRIMWADE ST., PRINCES ST., The Ancient House, UPPER ORWELL ST., PORTMAN ROAD, FRIARS STREET, FALCON ST., DOGS HEAD ST., TACKET ST., ORWELL PL., ROPE WALK, PORTMANS WALK, PRINCES STREET, ST. NICHOLAS ST., SILENT STREET, Bus Station, BROOK STREET, FOUNDATION STREET, WATERWORKS STREET, Police Headquarters Suffolk, Ipswich Town F.C., FRANCISCAN WAY, CUTLER ST., LOWER BROOK ST., LOWER ORWELL STREET, WATERWORKS ANGEL LA., GRIMWADE STREET, ST. PETER'S STREET, Wolsey's Gate, COLLEGE STREET, KEY STREET, SALTHOUSE ST., FORE STREET, A1156 TO FELIXSTOWE, WOLSEY STREET, COMMERCIAL ROAD, A137 TO HARWICH, RIVER ORWELL, Scale, Mile

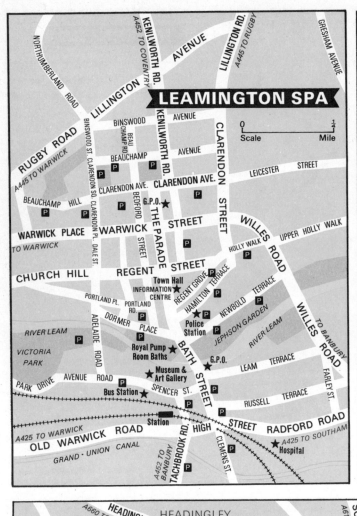

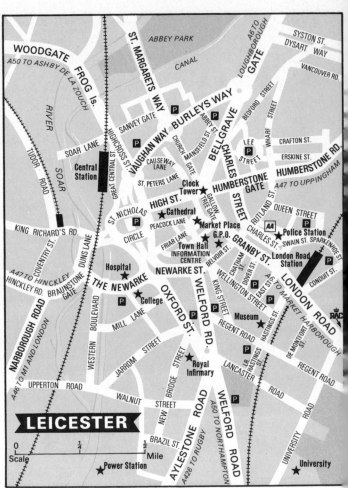

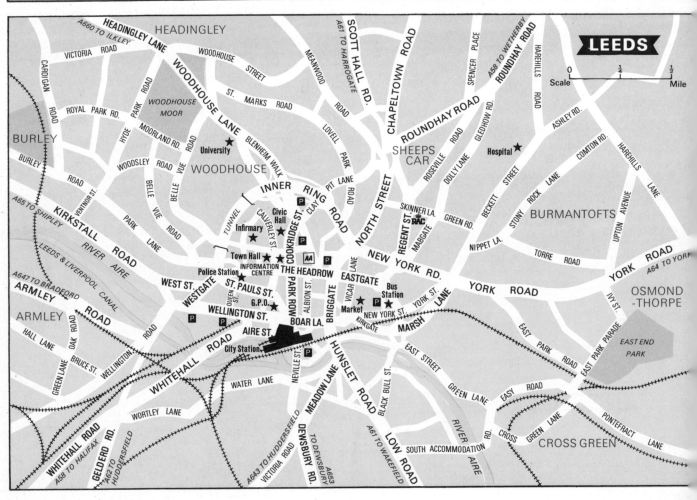

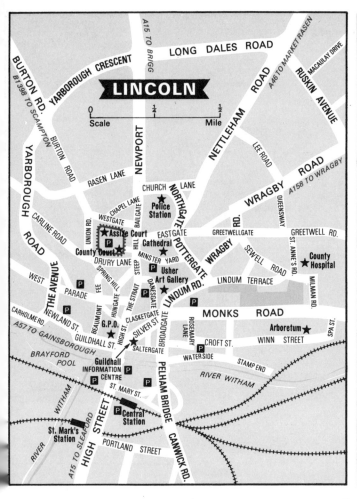

LINCOLN

Scale 0 ¼ ½ Mile

YARBOROUGH CRESCENT
LONG DALES ROAD
BURTON RD.
B1398 TO SCAMPTON
A15 TO BRIGG
RUSKIN AVENUE
A46 TO MARKET RASEN
MACAULAY DRIVE
NETTLEHAM ROAD
NEWPORT
RASEN LANE
LEE ROAD
CHURCH LANE
WRAGBY ROAD
QUEENSWAY
A158 TO WRAGBY
CHAPEL LANE
WESTGATE
BAILGATE
NORTHGATE
POTTERGATE
EASTGATE
GREETWELLGATE
GREETWELL RD.
UNION RD.
Assize Court
Cathedral
Police Station
ST. ANNE'S RD.
County Hospital
County Court
MINSTER YARD
DRURY LANE
SPRING HILL
STEEP HILL
Usher Art Gallery
LINDUM RD.
LINDUM TERRACE
SEWELL ROAD
MILMAN RD.
YARBOROUGH ROAD
CARLINE ROAD
THE AVENUE
WEST PARADE
BEAUMONT FEE
HUNGATE
THE STRAIT
DANESGATE
CLASKETGATE
MONKS ROAD
ROSEMARY LANE
WINN STREET
SPA RD.
Arboretum
NEWLAND ST.
CARHOLME RD.
A57 TO GAINSBOROUGH
GUILDHALL ST.
G.P.O.
HIGH ST.
SILVER ST.
SALTERGATE
BROADGATE
CROFT ST.
WATERSIDE
STAMP END
BRAYFORD POOL
Guildhall INFORMATION CENTRE
ST. MARY ST.
PELHAM BRIDGE
RIVER WITHAM
WITHAM
RIVER
HIGH STREET
Central Station
St. Mark's Station
A15 TO SLEAFORD
PORTLAND STREET
CANWICK RD.

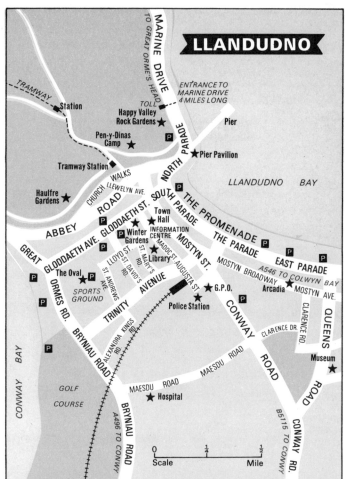

LLANDUDNO

MARINE DRIVE
TO GREAT ORME'S HEAD
ENTRANCE TO MARINE DRIVE 4 MILES LONG
TRAMWAY
Station
TOLL
Happy Valley Rock Gardens
Pier
Pen-y-Dinas Camp
Pier Pavilion
Tramway Station
NORTH PARADE
LLANDUDNO BAY
CHURCH WALKS
LLEWELYN AVE.
Haulfre Gardens
ABBEY ROAD
GREAT ORMES RD.
CHURCH ROAD
GLODDAETH ST.
GLODDAETH AVE.
SOUTH PARADE
THE PROMENADE
THE PARADE
EAST PARADE
Town Hall
Winter Gardens
LLOYD ST.
ST. MARY'S RD.
Information Centre
Library
MADOC ST.
ST. AUGUSTA ST.
MOSTYN ST.
MOSTYN BROADWAY
A546 TO COLWYN BAY
The Oval
ST. ANDREWS AVE.
ST. DAVID'S RD.
G.P.O.
Arcadia
MOSTYN AVE.
SPORTS GROUND
TRINITY AVENUE
Police Station
CONWAY ROAD
CLARENCE RD.
CLARENCE DR.
QUEENS ROAD
BRYNIAU ROAD
ALEXANDRA RD.
KINGS RD.
Museum
CONWAY BAY
MAESDU ROAD
MAESDU ROAD
GOLF COURSE
Hospital
B5115 TO CONWY
CONWY RD.
A496 TO CONWY
Scale 0 ¼ ½ Mile

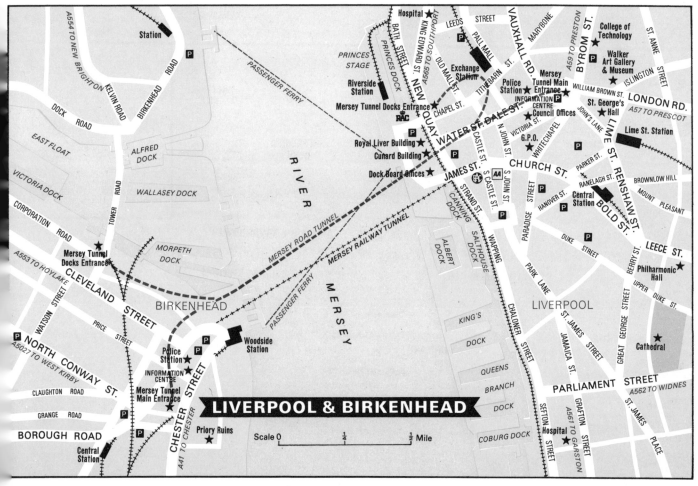

LIVERPOOL & BIRKENHEAD

Scale 0 ¼ ½ Mile

20

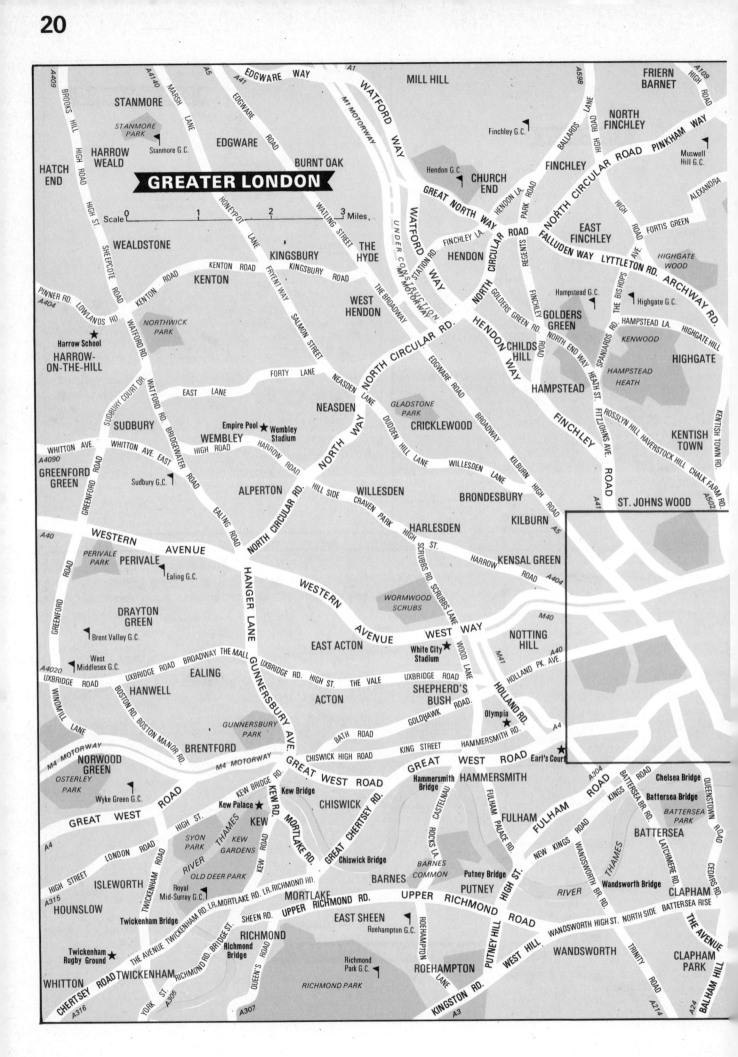

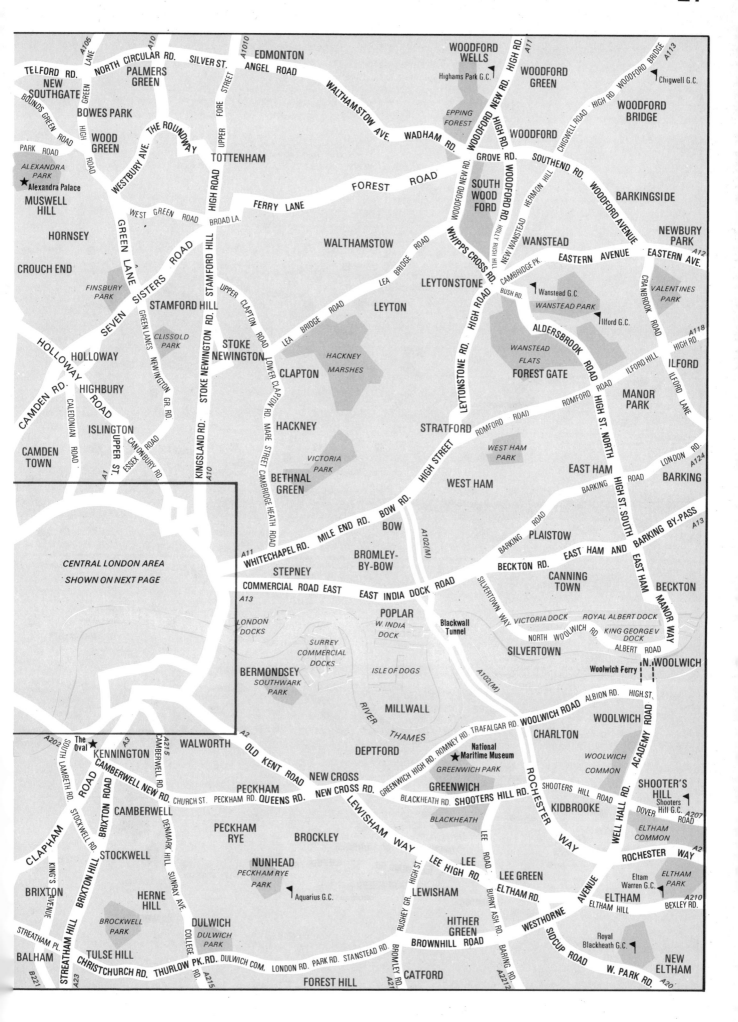

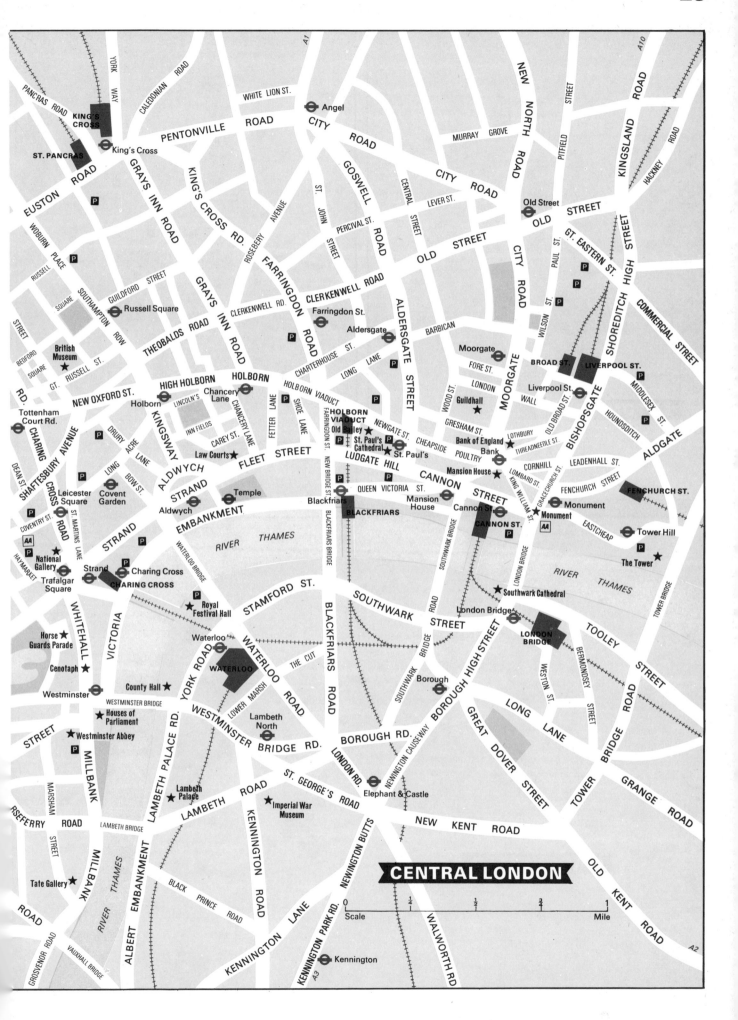

CENTRAL LONDON

Scale

0   ¼   ½   ¾   1   Mile

24

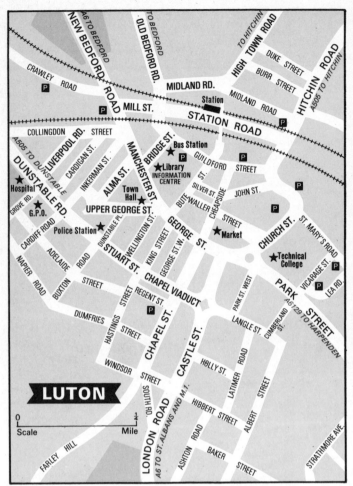

LUTON

Scale 0 ¼ Mile

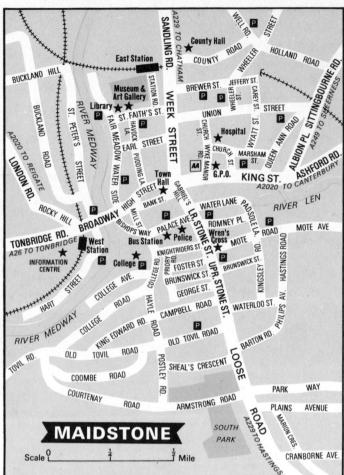

MAIDSTONE

Scale 0 ¼ ½ Mile

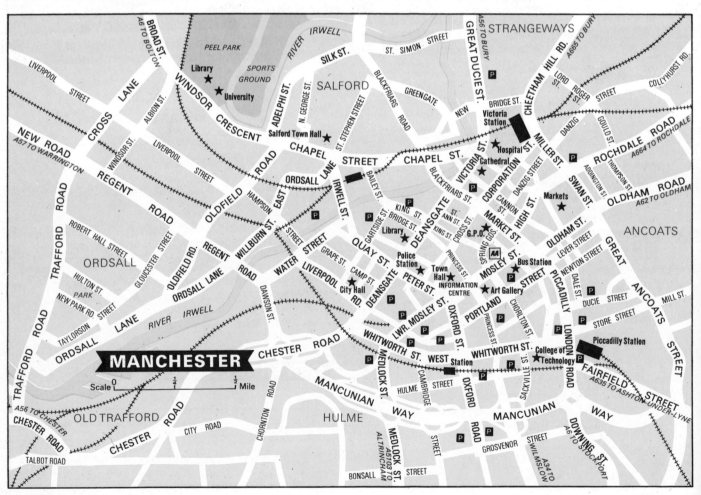

MANCHESTER

Scale 0 ¼ ½ Mile

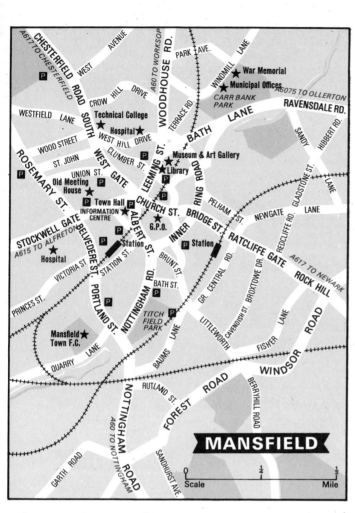

MANSFIELD

CHESTERFIELD ROAD SOUTH · A617 TO CHESTERFIELD
AVENUE
WEST
PARK AVE.
A60 TO WORKSOP
WINDMILL LANE
★ War Memorial
★ Municipal Offices
A5075 TO OLLERTON
WOODHOUSE RD.
PARK AVE.
WEST
CROW HILL DRIVE
WESTFIELD LANE
★ Technical College
★ Hospital ★
WEST HILL DRIVE
WOOD STREET
CLUMBER ST.
ST. JOHN
ROSEMARY ST.
WEST GATE
UNION ST.
Old Meeting House ★
LEEMING ST.
★ Museum & Art Gallery
★ Library
★ Town Hall
INFORMATION CENTRE
CHURCH ST.
★ Hospital
STOCKWELL GATE
A615 TO ALFRETON
BELVEDERE ST.
ALBERT ST.
G.P.O.
BRIDGE ST.
★ Station
INNER RING ROAD
RATCLIFFE GATE
ROCK HILL
A617 TO NEWARK
PRINCES ST.
VICTORIA ST.
STATION ST.
PORTLAND ST.
BATH ST.
BRUNT ST.
GR. CENTRAL RD.
CAVENDISH ST.
BROXTOWE DR.
TITCH FIELD PARK
LITTLEWORTH
FISHER
LANE
Mansfield Town F.C. ★
QUARRY LANE
BAUMS LANE
NOTTINGHAM RD.
RUTLAND ST.
FOREST ROAD
BERRYHILL ROAD
WINDSOR ROAD
GARTH ROAD
NOTTINGHAM ROAD A60 TO NOTTINGHAM
SANDHURST AVE.
Scale 0 ¼ ½ Mile
CARR BANK PARK
BATH LANE
WINDMILL LANE
TERRACE RD.
SANDY LANE
HIBBERT RD.
RAVENSDALE RD.
GLADSTONE ST.
REDCLIFFE RD.
NEWGATE LANE
PELHAM ST.

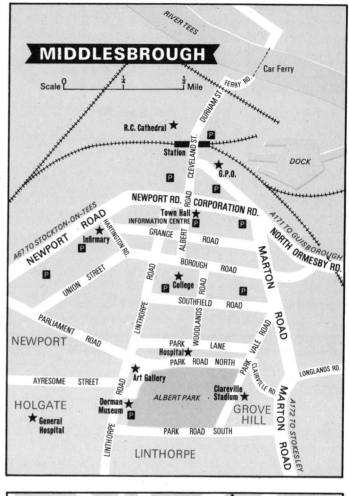

MIDDLESBROUGH

RIVER TEES
Car Ferry
Scale 0 ¼ ½ Mile
★ R.C. Cathedral ★
Station
DURHAM ROAD
FERRY RD.
CLEVELAND ST.
P
DOCK
G.P.O. ★
NEWPORT RD.
CORPORATION RD.
A171 TO GUISBOROUGH
A67 TO STOCKTON-ON-TEES
NEWPORT ROAD
HARTINGTON RD.
★ Town Hall
INFORMATION CENTRE
GRANGE ROAD
ALBERT ROAD
NORTH ORMESBY RD.
Infirmary ★
UNION STREET
BOROUGH ROAD
College ★
SOUTHFIELD ROAD
MARTON ROAD
LINTHORPE ROAD
WOODLANDS ROAD
VALE
NEWPORT
PARLIAMENT ROAD
PARK LANE
Park Hospital ★
PARK ROAD NORTH
CLAIRVILLE RD.
MARTON ROAD
LONGLANDS RD.
AYRESOME STREET
★ Art Gallery
ALBERT PARK
Clareville Stadium ★
GROVE HILL
A172 TO STOKESLEY
HOLGATE
Dorman Museum ★
P
★ General Hospital
PARK ROAD SOUTH
LINTHORPE

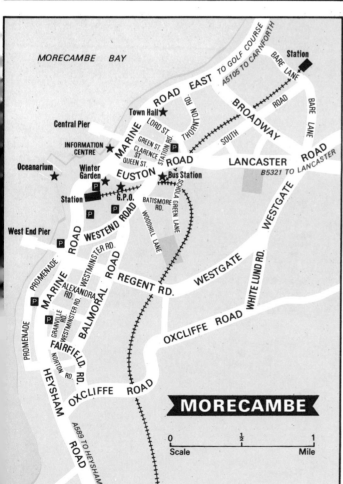

MORECAMBE

MORECAMBE BAY
Station
TO GOLF COURSE
A5105 TO CARNFORTH
BARE LANE
ROAD EAST
BROADWAY
BARE LANE
Central Pier
Town Hall ★
MARINE ROAD
LORD ST.
THORNTON RD.
SOUTH ROAD
INFORMATION CENTRE ★
GREEN ST.
CLARENCE ST.
STATION RD.
LANCASTER ROAD
B5321 TO LANCASTER
WESTGATE ROAD
Oceanarium ★
Winter Garden ★
QUEEN ST.
Euston ★
Bus Station ★
SCHOLA GREEN LANE
Station
G.P.O.
BATISMORE RD.
WOODHILL LANE
West End Pier ★
WESTEND ROAD
WESTMINSTER RD.
MARINE ROAD
REGENT RD.
WESTGATE
OXCLIFFE ROAD
WHITE LUND RD.
PROMENADE
ALEXANDRA RD.
BALMORAL ROAD
GRANVILLE RD.
WESTMINSTER RD.
FAIRFIELD RD.
NORTON RD.
HEYSHAM ROAD
OXCLIFFE ROAD
A589 TO HEYSHAM
Scale 0 ½ 1 Mile

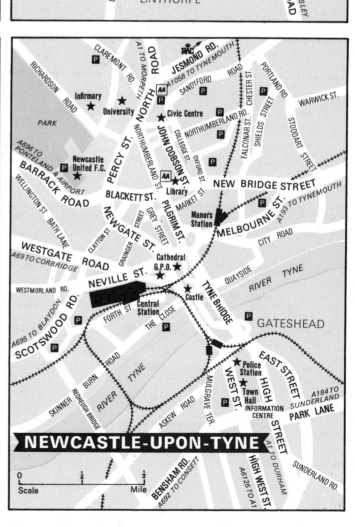

NEWCASTLE-UPON-TYNE

CLAREMONT RD.
RAC
JESMOND RD.
A1058 TO TYNEMOUTH
A1 TO MORPETH
RICHARDSON RD.
SANDYFORD ROAD
PORTLAND RD.
WARWICK ST.
PARK
Infirmary ★
★ University
AA
NORTH ROAD
PERCY ST.
Civic Centre ★
NORTHUMBERLAND RD.
CHESTER ST.
STODDART STREET
A696 TO PONTELAND & AIRPORT
Newcastle United F.C. ★
JOHN DOBSON ST.
COLLEGE ST.
OXFORD ST.
FALCONAR ST.
SHIELDS STREET
NEW BRIDGE STREET
BARRACK ROAD
AA
Library ★
BLACKETT ST.
PILGRIM ST.
MARKET ST.
Manors Station ↓
MELBOURNE ST.
A193 TO TYNEMOUTH
WELLINGTON ST.
BATH LANE
NEWGATE ST.
CLAYTON ST.
GRAINGER ST.
GREY STREET
CITY ROAD
WESTGATE ROAD
A69 TO CORBRIDGE
Cathedral ★
G.P.O. ★
QUAYSIDE
RIVER TYNE
WESTMORLAND RD.
NEVILLE ST.
Castle ★
TYNE BRIDGE
A695 TO BLAYDON
SCOTSWOOD ROAD
P
FORTH ST.
Central Station
THE CLOSE
GATESHEAD
REDHEUGH BRIDGE
SKINNER BURN ROAD
RIVER TYNE
ASKEW ROAD
MULGRAVE TER.
★ Police Station
WEST ST.
HIGH STREET
★ Town Hall
INFORMATION CENTRE
EAST STREET
A184 TO SUNDERLAND
PARK LANE
BENSHAM RD.
A692 TO CONSETT
HIGH WEST ST.
A1 TO DURHAM
A6125 TO A1
SUNDERLAND RD.
Scale 0 ¼ ½ Mile

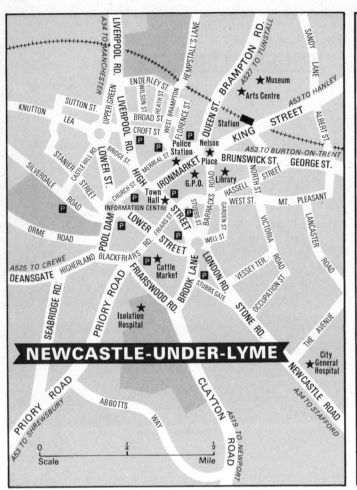

NEWCASTLE-UNDER-LYME

A34 TO MANCHESTER
LIVERPOOL RD.
KNUTTON
SUTTON ST.
LEA
UPPER GREEN
ENDERLEY ST.
WILSON ST.
HEATH ST.
WEST BRAMPTON
BROAD ST.
FLORENCE ST.
CROFT ST.
HEMPSTALL'S LANE
QUEEN ST.
BRAMPTON RD.
A527 TO TUNSTALL
SANDY LANE
★ Museum
★ Arts Centre
A53 TO HANLEY
ALBERT ST.
KING STREET
Station
STANIER ST.
CASTLE HILL RD.
LIVERPOOL RD.
BRIDGE ST.
LOWER ST.
HIGH STREET
CHURCH ST.
MERRIAL ST.
IRONMARKET
★ Nelson Place
Police Station
BRUNSWICK ST.
NORTH ST.
A52 TO BURTON-ON-TRENT
GEORGE ST.
SILVERDALE ROAD
ORME ROAD
POOL DAM
★ Town Hall
INFORMATION CENTRE
G.P.O.
Library
HASSELL ST.
WEST ST.
MT. PLEASANT
LANCASTER ROAD
STUBBS ST.
BARRACKS RD.
GARDEN ST.
WELL ST.
VICTORIA ROAD
DEANSGATE
SEABRIDGE RD.
HIGHERLAND
BLACKFRIARS
A525 TO CREWE
PRIORY ROAD
FRIARS RD.
LOWER STREET
FRIARSWOOD RD.
★ Cattle Market
BROOK LANE
STUBBS GATE
LONDON RD.
STONE RD.
OCCUPATION ST.
VESSEY TER.
★ Isolation Hospital
THE AVENUE
NEW CASTLE ROAD
★ City General Hospital
A34 TO STAFFORD
PRIORY ROAD
A53 TO SHREWSBURY
ABBOTTS WAY
CLAYTON ROAD
A519 TO NEWPORT

0   ¼   ½
Scale   Mile

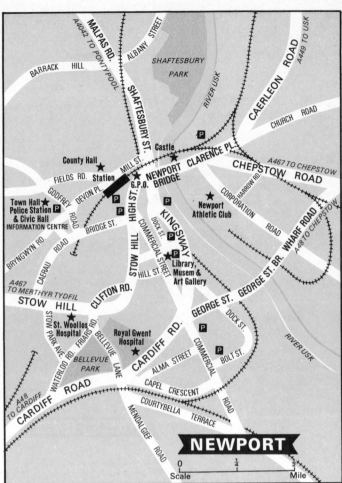

NEWPORT

A4042 TO PONTYPOOL
MALPAS RD.
BARRACK HILL
ALBANY STREET
SHAFTESBURY PARK
CAERLEON ROAD
A449 TO USK
SHAFTESBURY ST.
River Usk
CHURCH ROAD
County Hall ★
MILL ST.
Castle ★
★ Station
FIELDS RD.
Newport CLARENCE PL.
NEWPORT BRIDGE
G.P.O.
CHEPSTOW ROAD
A467 TO CHEPSTOW
GODFREY RD.
DEVON PL.
HIGH ST.
★ Town Hall
Police Station
& Civic Hall
INFORMATION CENTRE
BRYNGWYN RD.
CAERAU ROAD
BRIDGE ST.
STOW HILL
COMMERCIAL STREET
DOCK ST.
KINGSWAY
CORPORATION
HARROW RD.
★ Newport Athletic Club
ROAD
GEORGE ST. BR.
WHARF ROAD
A48 TO CHEPSTOW
A467 TO MERTHYR TYDFIL
STOW HILL
CLIFTON RD.
HILL ST.
★ Library, Musem & Art Gallery
GEORGE ST.
DOCK ST.
RIVER USK
STOW PARK AVE.
★ St. Woollos Hospital
WATERLOO RD.
FRIARS RD.
BELLEVUE LANE
CARDIFF RD.
CARDIFF ROAD
★ Royal Gwent Hospital
BELLEVUE PARK
ALMA STREET
COMMERCIAL ROAD
BOLT ST.
A48 TO CARDIFF
CAPEL CRESCENT
MENDALGIEF ROAD
COURTYBELLA TERRACE

0   ¼   ½
Scale   Mile

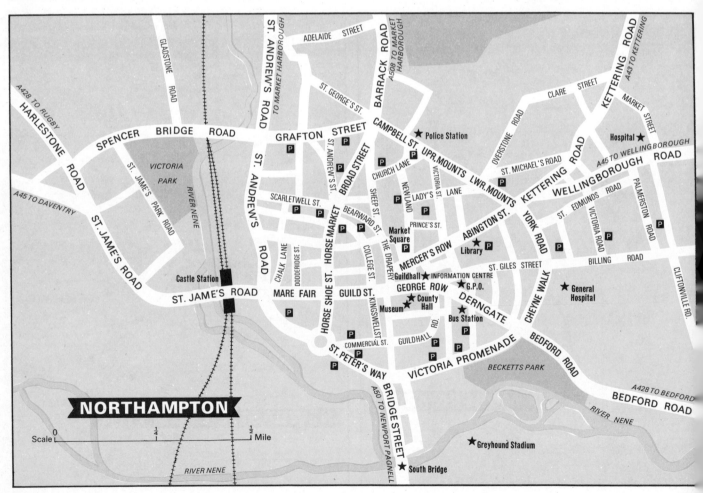

NORTHAMPTON

A428 TO RUGBY
HARLESTONE ROAD
GLADSTONE ROAD
ST. ANDREW'S ROAD
TO MARKET HARBOROUGH
ADELAIDE STREET
BARRACK ROAD
A508 TO MARKET HARBOROUGH
KETTERING ROAD
A43 TO KETTERING
MARKET STREET
SPENCER BRIDGE ROAD
GRAFTON STREET
ST. GEORGE'S ST.
CLARE STREET
★ Hospital
A45 TO DAVENTRY
VICTORIA PARK
ST. JAMES'S PARK ROAD
RIVER NENE
ST. ANDREW'S ROAD
ST. ANDREW'S ST.
BROAD STREET
CAMPBELL ST.
UPR. MOUNTS
★ Police Station
OVERSTONE RD.
ST. MICHAEL'S ROAD
KETTERING ROAD
A45 TO WELLINGBOROUGH
WELLINGBOROUGH ROAD
ST. JAMES'S ROAD
SCARLETWELL ST.
CHURCH LANE
NEWLAND
LADY'S LANE
LWR. MOUNTS
VICTORIA ST.
ABINGTON ST.
YORK ROAD
ST. EDMUNDS
VICTORIA ROAD
PALMERSTON ROAD
BILLING ROAD
Castle Station
ST. JAMES'S ROAD
MARE FAIR
CHALK LANE
DODDRIDGE ST.
HORSE MARKET
HORSE SHOE ST.
BEARWARD ST.
SHEEP ST.
PRINCE'S ST.
THE DRAPERY
★ Market Square
MERCER'S ROW
Library
ST. GILES STREET
CHEYNE WALK
★ General Hospital
CLIFTONVILLE RD.
GUILD ST.
COLLEGE ST.
KINGSWELL ST.
Guildhall ★
INFORMATION CENTRE
GEORGE ROW
★ G.P.O.
★ Museum
★ County Hall
DERNGATE
COMMERCIAL ST.
GUILDHALL RD.
Bus Station
ST. PETER'S WAY
VICTORIA PROMENADE
BEDFORD ROAD
BECKETTS PARK
A428 TO BEDFORD
BEDFORD ROAD
BRIDGE STREET
A60 TO NEWPORT PAGNELL
★ Greyhound Stadium
★ South Bridge
RIVER NENE

0   ¼   ½
Scale   Mile

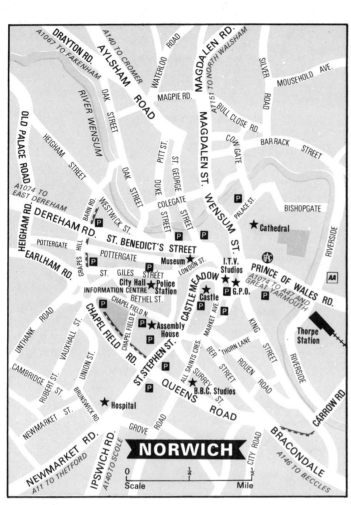

NORWICH

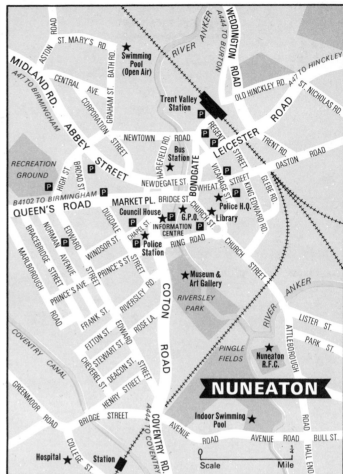

NUNEATON

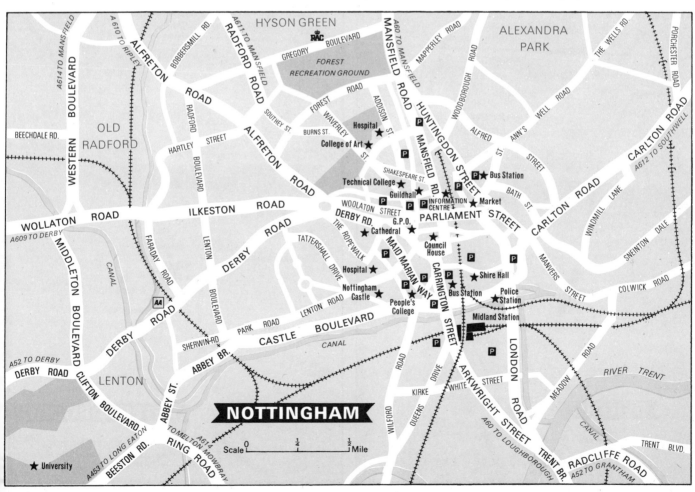

NOTTINGHAM

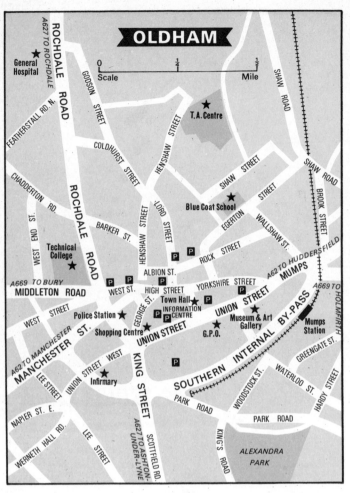

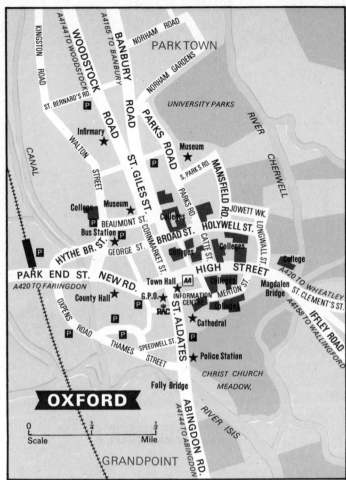

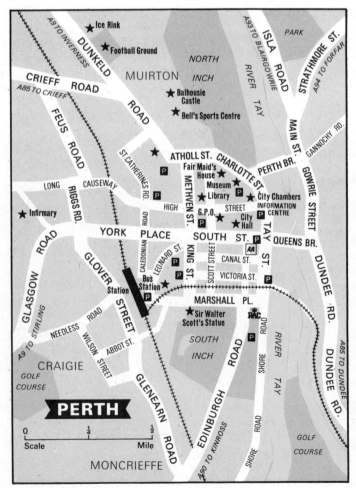

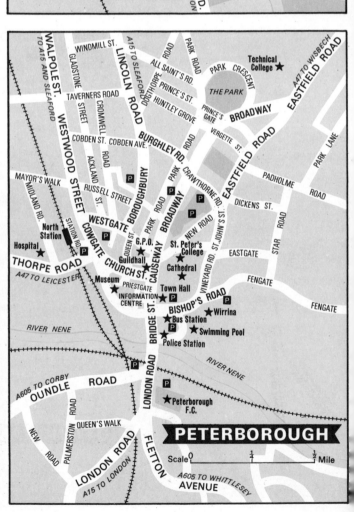

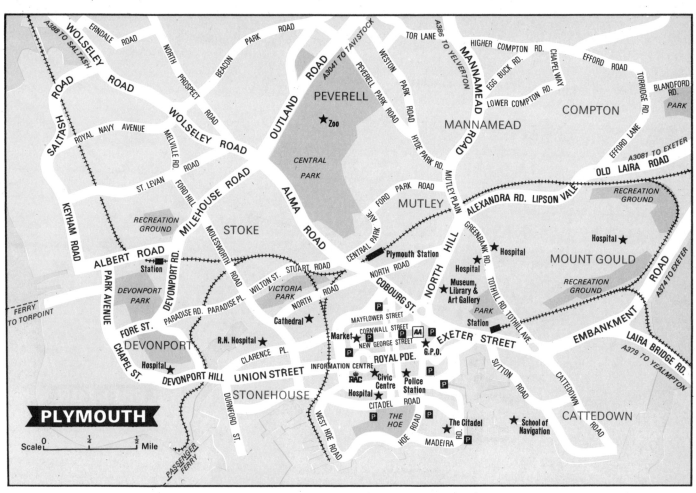

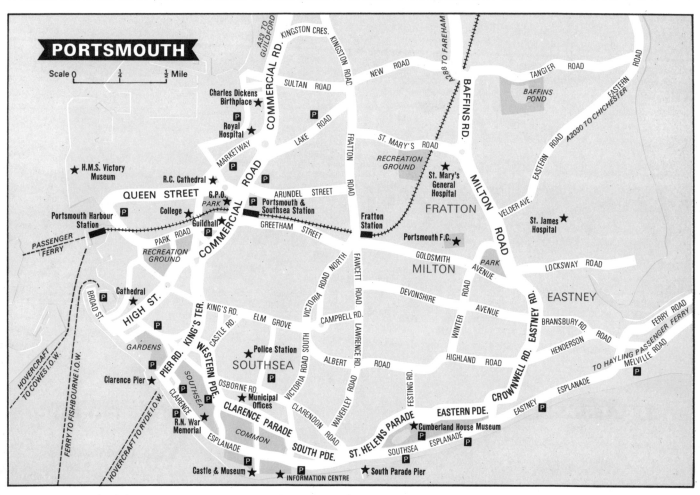

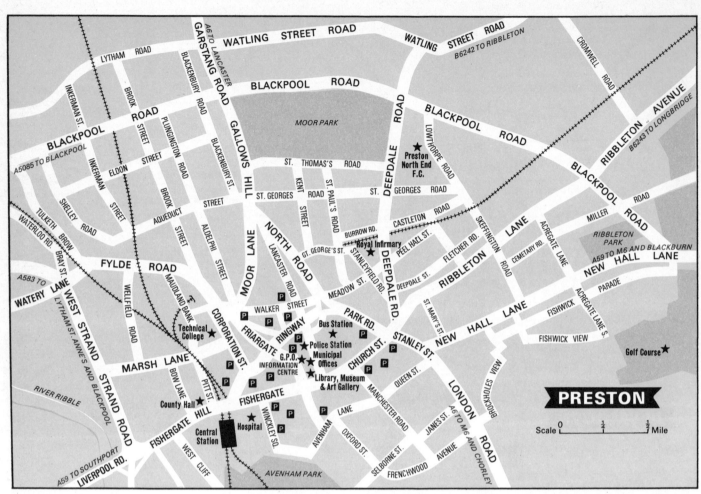

PRESTON

Scale 0   ¼   ½ Mile

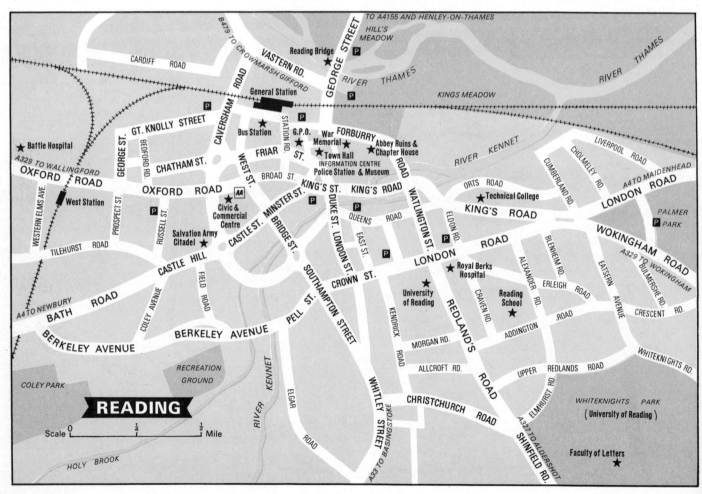

READING

Scale 0   ¼   ½ Mile

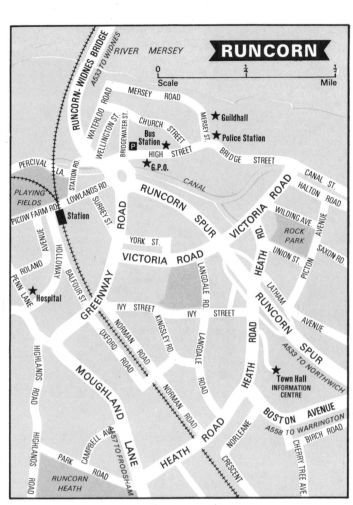

RUNCORN

Scale 0 ¼ ½ Mile

RIVER MERSEY

RUNCORN-WIDNES BRIDGE
A533 TO WIDNES
MERSEY ROAD
WATERLOO ROAD
WELLINGTON ST.
BRIDGEWATER ST.
CHURCH STREET
MERSEY ST.
Guildhall
Police Station
Bus Station
HIGH STREET
BRIDGE STREET
G.P.O.
CANAL
PERCIVAL LA.
PLAYING FIELDS
PICOW FARM RD.
LOWLANDS RD.
STATION RD.
SURREY ST.
Station
CANAL ST.
HALTON ROAD
VICTORIA ROAD
WILDING AVE.
AVENUE
ROCK PARK
UNION ST.
PICTON
SAXON RD.
RUNCORN SPUR
YORK ST.
VICTORIA ROAD
HOLLOWAY
AVENUE
ROLAND
PENN LANE
BALFOUR ST.
GREENWAY ROAD
NORMAN ROAD
OXFORD ROAD
KINGSLEY RD.
IVY STREET
IVY STREET
LANGDALE RD.
LANGDALE
HEATH ROAD
LATHAM AVENUE
RUNCORN SPUR
A533 TO NORTHWICH
Hospital
MOUGHLAND LANE
NORMAN ROAD
HIGHLANDS ROAD
HIGHLANDS ROAD
CAMPBELL AVE.
A557 TO FRODSHAM
PARK ROAD
RUNCORN HEATH
HEATH ROAD
NORLEANE CRESCENT
Town Hall INFORMATION CENTRE
BOSTON AVENUE
A558 TO WARRINGTON
BIRCH ROAD
CHERRY TREE AVE.

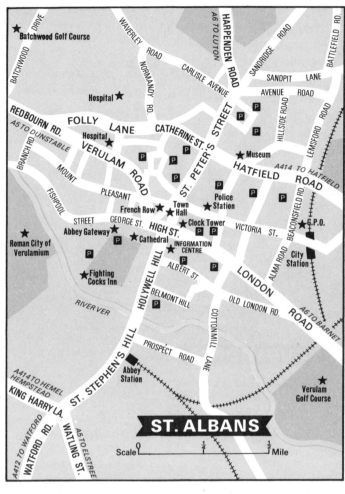

ST. ALBANS

Scale ¼ ½ Mile

Batchwood Golf Course
BATCHWOOD DRIVE
WAVERLEY ROAD
NORMANDY RD.
A6 TO LUTON
HARPENDEN ROAD
CARLISLE AVENUE
SANDRIDGE ROAD
SANDPIT LANE
BATTLEFIELD RD.
Hospital
REDBOURN RD.
A5 TO DUNSTABLE
FOLLY LANE
CATHERINE ST.
ST. PETER'S STREET
AVENUE ROAD
HILLSIDE ROAD
LEMSFORD ROAD
Hospital
BRANCH RD.
VERULAM ROAD
MOUNT PLEASANT
FISHPOOL STREET
Museum
HATFIELD ROAD
A414 TO HATFIELD
BEACONSFIELD RD.
Roman City of Verulamium
French Row
Town Hall
Police Station
ALMA ROAD
G.P.O.
Abbey Gateway
GEORGE ST.
HIGH ST.
Clock Tower
Cathedral
VICTORIA ST.
INFORMATION CENTRE
City Station
A6 TO BARNET
Fighting Cocks Inn
ALBERT ST.
HOLYWELL HILL
BELMONT HILL
OLD LONDON RD.
LONDON ROAD
RIVER VER
COTTONMILL LANE
ST. STEPHEN'S HILL
PROSPECT ROAD
A414 TO HEMEL HEMPSTEAD
KING HARRY LA.
Abbey Station
Verulam Golf Course
A412 TO WATFORD
WATFORD RD.
WATLING ST.
A5 TO ELSTREE

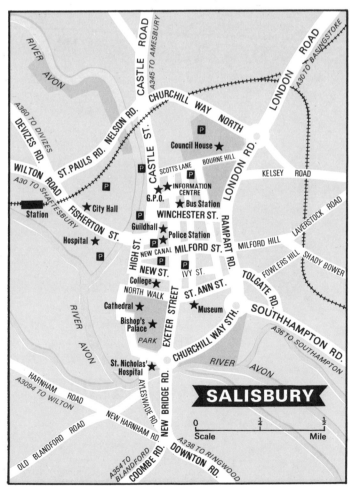

SALISBURY

Scale 0 ¼ Mile

RIVER AVON
CASTLE ROAD
A345 TO AMESBURY
CHURCHILL WAY NORTH
LONDON ROAD
A30 TO BASINGSTOKE
A360 TO DEVIZES
DEVIZES ROAD
ST. PAULS RD.
NELSON RD.
CASTLE ST.
Council House
SCOTTS LANE
BOURNE HILL
KELSEY ROAD
WILTON ROAD
A30 TO SHAFTESBURY
Station
FISHERTON ST.
INFORMATION CENTRE
G.P.O.
Bus Station
WINCHESTER ST.
RAMPART RD.
LAVERSTOCK ROAD
City Hall
Guildhall
Police Station
MILFORD ST.
MILFORD HILL
FOWLERS HILL
SHADY BOWER
Hospital
HIGH ST.
NEW CANAL
IVY ST.
NEW ST.
College
NORTH WALK
EXETER STREET
ST. ANN ST.
TOLGATE RD.
Cathedral
Museum
Bishop's Palace
Park
CHURCHILL WAY STH.
SOUTHAMPTON RD.
A36 TO SOUTHAMPTON
RIVER AVON
St. Nicholas' Hospital
RIVER AVON
HARNHAM ROAD
A3094 TO WILTON
AYLESWADE RD.
NEW BRIDGE RD.
NEW HARNHAM RD.
A338 TO RINGWOOD
OLD BLANDFORD ROAD
A354 TO BLANDFORD
COOMBE RD.
BLANDFORD RD.
DOWNTON RD.

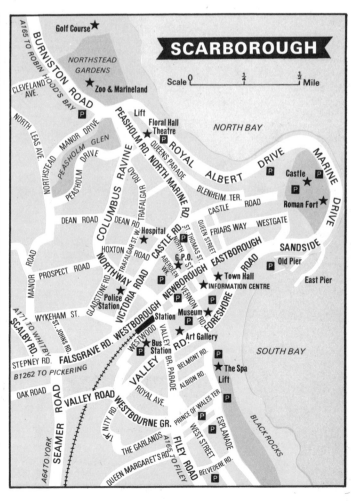

SCARBOROUGH

Scale 0 ¼ ½ Mile

Golf Course
A165 TO ROBIN HOOD'S BAY
BURNISTON ROAD
NORTHSTEAD GARDENS
CLEVELAND AVE.
Zoo & Marineland
Lift
Floral Hall Theatre
NORTH BAY
NORTH LEAS AVE.
NORTHSTEAD MANOR DRIVE
PEASHOLM GLEN
PEASHOLM DRIVE
PEASHOLM RD.
ROYAL ALBERT DRIVE
QUEENS PARADE
Lift
MARINE DRIVE
TRAFALGAR ROAD
NORTH MARINE RD.
BLENHEIM TER.
Castle
Roman Fort
COLUMBUS RAVINE
DEAN ROAD
DEAN RD.
TRAFALGAR SQUARE
CASTLE ROAD
Hospital
CASTLE RD.
FRIARS WAY
WESTGATE
SANDSIDE
HOXTON ROAD
QUEEN STREET
ST. THOMAS ST.
EASTBOROUGH
Old Pier
PROSPECT ROAD
ABERDEEN WK.
G.P.O.
NEWBOROUGH
East Pier
NORTHWAY
GLADSTONE ROAD
VICTORIA ROAD
Town Hall
MANOR ROAD
A171 TO WHITBY
SCALBY RD.
WYKEHAM ST.
Police Station
VERNON RD.
INFORMATION CENTRE
FORESHORE ROAD
ST. JOHNS RD.
WESTBOROUGH
Station
Museum
SOUTH BAY
STEPNEY RD.
FALSGRAVE RD.
Bus Station
Art Gallery
B1262 TO PICKERING
WESTWOOD
VALLEY RD.
SEAMER ROAD
A64 TO YORK
VALLEY
The Spa
Lift
VALLEY BR.
BELMONT RD.
VALLEY ROAD
WESTBOURNE GR.
ALBION RD.
OAK ROAD
TRINITY RD.
ROYAL AVE.
PRINCE OF WALES TER.
ESPLANADE
BLACK ROCKS
THE GARLANDS
WEST STREET
FILEY ROAD
A165 TO FILEY
BELVEDERE RD.
QUEEN MARGARET'S RD.
WESTBOURNE

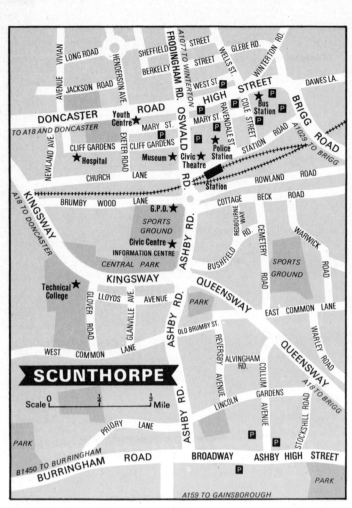

SCUNTHORPE

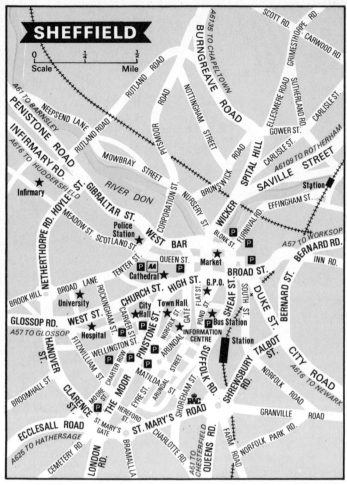

SHEFFIELD

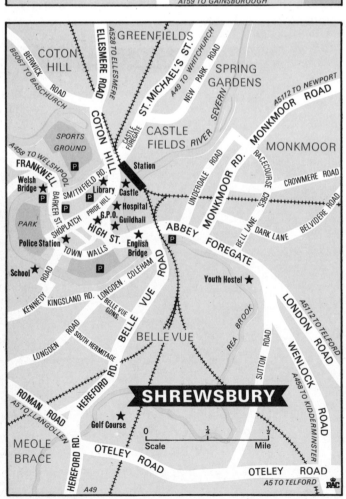

SHREWSBURY

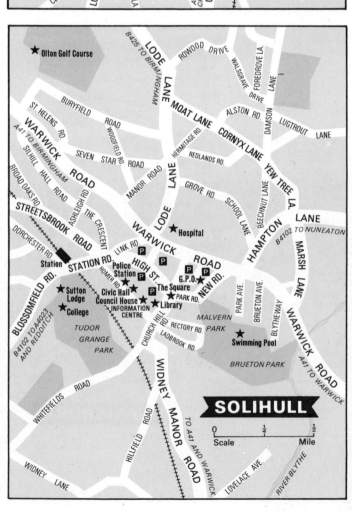

SOLIHULL

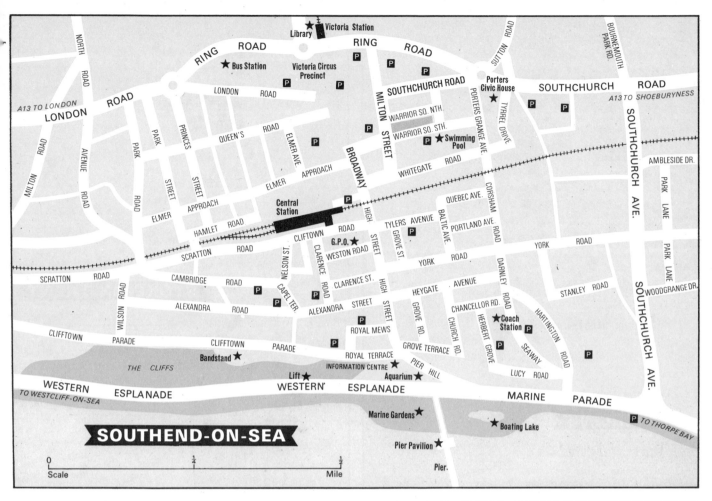

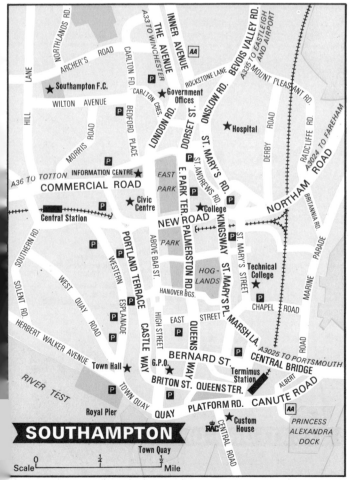

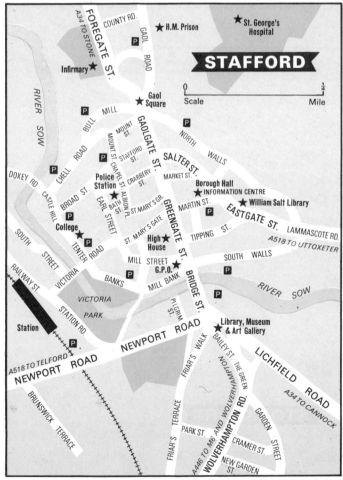

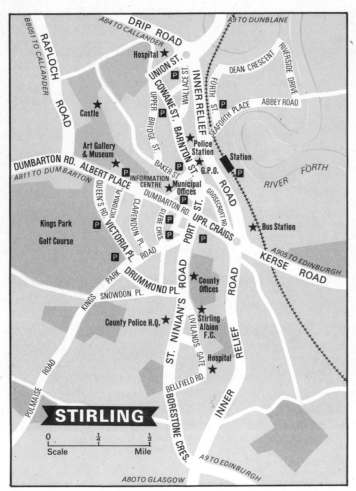

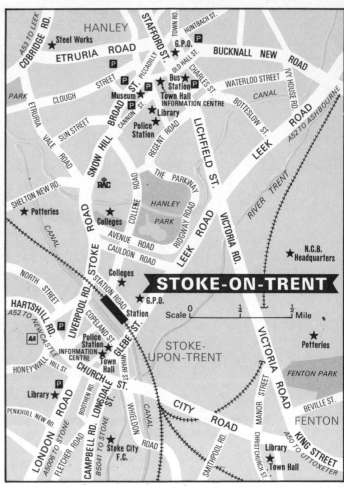

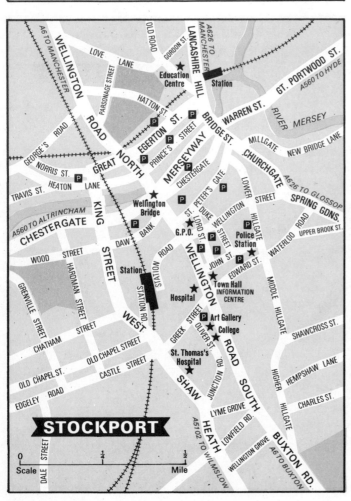

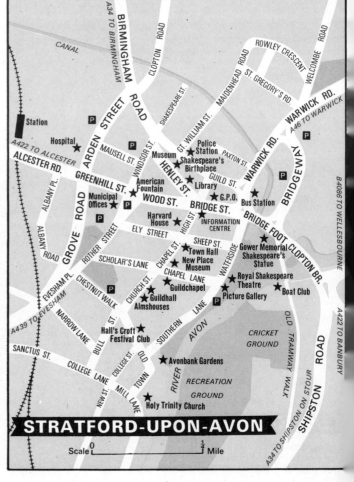

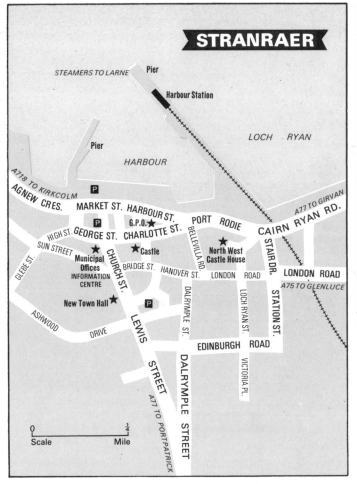

STRANRAER

STEAMERS TO LARNE · Pier
Harbour Station
LOCH RYAN
Pier
HARBOUR
A718 TO KIRKCOLM
AGNEW CRES.
MARKET ST. HARBOUR ST.
PORT RODIE
CAIRN RYAN RD.
A77 TO GIRVAN
G.P.O.
HIGH ST. GEORGE ST. CHARLOTTE ST.
BELLEVILLA RD.
STAIR DR.
LONDON ROAD
SUN STREET
★ Castle
North West
Castle House
LONDON ROAD
A75 TO GLENLUCE
GLEBE ST.
CHURCH ST.
Municipal
Offices
INFORMATION
CENTRE
BRIDGE ST.
HANOVER RD.
New Town Hall ★
ASHWOOD
DRIVE
LEWIS
STREET
DALRYMPLE ST.
LOCH RYAN ST.
EDINBURGH ROAD
VICTORIA PL.
STATION ST.
DALRYMPLE
STREET
A77 TO PORTPATRICK
0   1/4
Scale   Mile

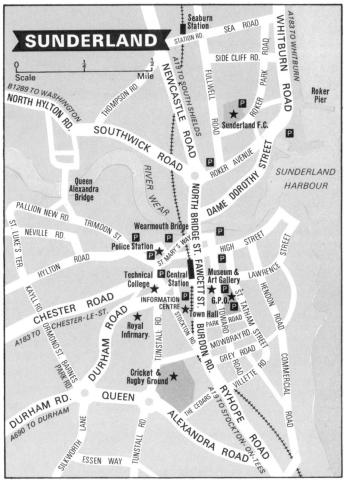

SUNDERLAND

Seaburn Station
STATION RD.
SEA ROAD
WHITBURN ROAD
A183 TO WHITBURN
0   1/4   1/2
Scale   Mile
B1289 TO WASHINGTON
A19 TO SOUTH SHIELDS
SIDE CLIFF RD.
NORTH HYLTON RD.
THOMPSON RD.
SOUTHWICK ROAD
NEWCASTLE ROAD
FULLWELL
ROKER PARK ROAD
Roker Pier
★ Sunderland F.C.
Queen
Alexandra
Bridge
RIVER WEAR
ROKER AVENUE
NORTH BRIDGE ST.
DAME DOROTHY STREET
SUNDERLAND HARBOUR
PALLION NEW RD.
TRIMDON ST.
Wearmouth Bridge
ST. LUKE'S TER.
NEVILLE RD.
Police Station ★
ST. MARY'S WAY
HIGH STREET
LAWRENCE
HYLTON ROAD
Technical College
Central Station
FAWCETT ST.
Museum & Art Gallery ★
HENDON ROAD
COMMERCIAL
STREET
KAYLL RD.
CHESTER ROAD
INFORMATION CENTRE
G.P.O.
ST. TATHAM STREET
A183 TO CHESTER-LE-ST.
DURHAM ROAD
Royal Infirmary
Town Hall
TOWARD PARK ROAD
MOWBRAY RD.
GREY ROAD
VILLETTE RD.
ROAD
BARNES PARK RD.
STOCKTON RD.
BURDON RD.
RYHOPE ROAD
A183 TO ORMOND ST.
TUNSTALL RD.
Cricket & Rugby Ground ★
THE CEDARS
A19 TO STOCKTON
DURHAM RD.
A690 TO DURHAM
QUEEN
SILKWORTH LANE
ESSEN WAY
TUNSTALL LANE
ALEXANDRA ROAD
A19 TO STOCKTON-ON-TEES

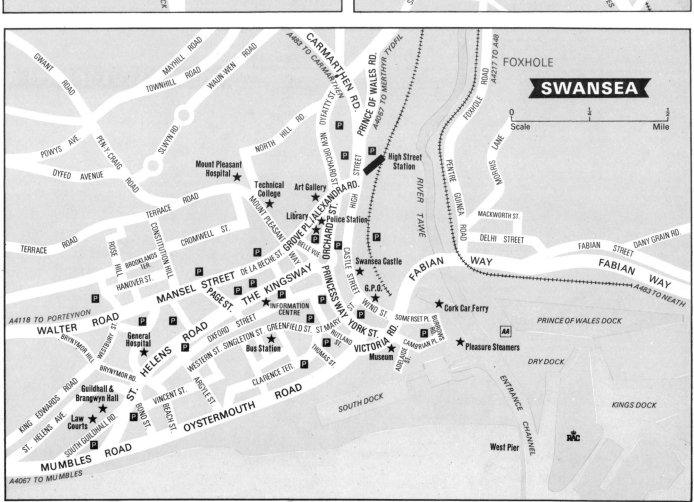

SWANSEA

GWANT ROAD
MAYHILL ROAD
WAUN WEN ROAD
CARMARTHEN RD.
A483 TO CARMARTHEN
PRINCE OF WALES RD.
A4067 TO MERTHYR TYDFIL
A4217 TO A48
FOXHOLE
TOWNHILL ROAD
DYFATTY ST.
0   1/4   1/2
Scale   Mile
POWYS AVE.
PEN-Y-CRAIG ROAD
SLWYN RD.
NORTH HILL RD.
NEW ORCHARD STREET
HIGH STREET
FOXHOLE ROAD
DYFED AVENUE
High Street Station
RIVER TAWE
PENTRE GUINEA ROAD
MORRIS LANE
Mount Pleasant Hospital ★
Technical College ★
Art Gallery ★
ALEXANDRA RD.
MACKWORTH ST.
TERRACE ROAD
MOUNT PLEASANT
Library ★
GROVE PL.
ORCHARD ST.
Police Station ★
HIGH STREET
DELHI STREET
FABIAN STREET
DANY GRAIN RD.
TERRACE ROAD
ROSE HILL
BROOKLANDS TER.
CROMWELL ST.
BELLE VUE
CASTLE STREET
Swansea Castle ★
FABIAN WAY
FABIAN WAY
A483 TO NEATH
CONSTITUTION HILL
HANOVER ST.
MANSEL STREET
PAGE ST.
THE KINGSWAY
PRINCESS WAY
G.P.O. ★
WIND ST.
A4118 TO PORTEYNON
WALTER ROAD
General Hospital ★
INFORMATION CENTRE
YORK ST.
SOMERSET PL.
BURROWS RD.
Cork Car Ferry ★
PRINCE OF WALES DOCK
BRYNMOR HILL
WESTBURY ST.
OXFORD STREET
WESTERN ST. SINGLETON ST. GREENFIELD ST.
ST. MARY ST.
RUTLAND ST.
VICTORIA RD.
CAMBRIAN PL.
AA
Pleasure Steamers ★
DRY DOCK
ST. HELENS ROAD
Bus Station ★
THOMAS ST.
Museum ★
ADELAIDE ST.
BRYNMOR RD.
CLARENCE TER.
ENTRANCE CHANNEL
KINGS DOCK
KING EDWARDS ROAD
Guildhall & Brangwyn Hall ★
VINCENT ST.
ARGYLE ST.
BEACH ST.
BOND ST.
OYSTERMOUTH ROAD
SOUTH DOCK
ST. HELENS AVE.
Law Courts ★
SOUTH GUILDHALL RD.
West Pier
RAC
MUMBLES ROAD
A4067 TO MUMBLES

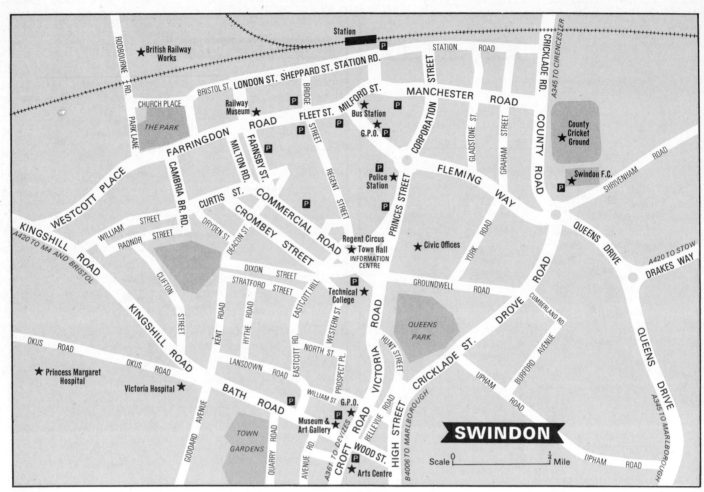

SWINDON

Scale 0 |_____| 1/4 Mile

British Railway Works
Station
STATION ROAD
CRICKLADE RD.
A345 TO CIRENCESTER
RODBOURNE RD.
BRISTOL ST.
LONDON ST.
SHEPPARD ST.
STATION RD.
MANCHESTER ROAD
County Cricket Ground
CHURCH PLACE
Railway Museum
FLEET ST.
MILFORD ST.
CORPORATION STREET
GLADSTONE ST.
GRAHAM STREET
COUNTY ROAD
Swindon F.C.
SHRIVENHAM ROAD
THE PARK
PARK LANE
FARRINGDON ROAD
Bus Station
G.P.O.
PRINCES STREET
FLEMING WAY
CAMBRIA BR. RD.
FARNSBY ST.
BRIDGE STREET
REGENT STREET
Police Station
YORK ROAD
QUEENS DRIVE
WESTCOTT PLACE
MILTON RD.
CURTIS ST.
COMMERCIAL ROAD
CROMBEY STREET
DRYDEN ST.
DEACON ST.
Regent Circus
Town Hall INFORMATION CENTRE
Civic Offices
GROUNDWELL ROAD
DROVE ROAD
QUEENS DRIVE
A420 TO STOW
DRAKES WAY
KINGSHILL ROAD
A420 TO M4 AND BRISTOL
WILLIAM STREET
RADNOR STREET
CLIFTON STREET
DIXON STREET
STRATFORD STREET
EASTCOTT HILL
WESTERN ST.
Technical College
VICTORIA ROAD
HUNT STREET
Queens Park
CUMBERLAND RD.
A345 TO MARLBOROUGH
KINGSHILL ROAD
KENT ROAD
HYTHE ROAD
NORTH ST.
PROSPECT PL.
CRICKLADE ST.
UPHAM ROAD
BURFORD AVENUE
OKUS ROAD
OKUS ROAD
LANSDOWN ROAD
EASTCOTT RD.
WILLIAM ST.
G.P.O.
BELLEVUE ROAD
HIGH STREET
B4006 TO MARLBOROUGH
Princess Margaret Hospital
Victoria Hospital
BATH ROAD
GODDARD AVENUE
QUARRY ROAD
Museum & Art Gallery
CROFT ROAD
WOOD ST.
AVENUE RD.
A361 TO DEVIZES
TOWN GARDENS
Arts Centre
QUEENS DRIVE
UPHAM ROAD

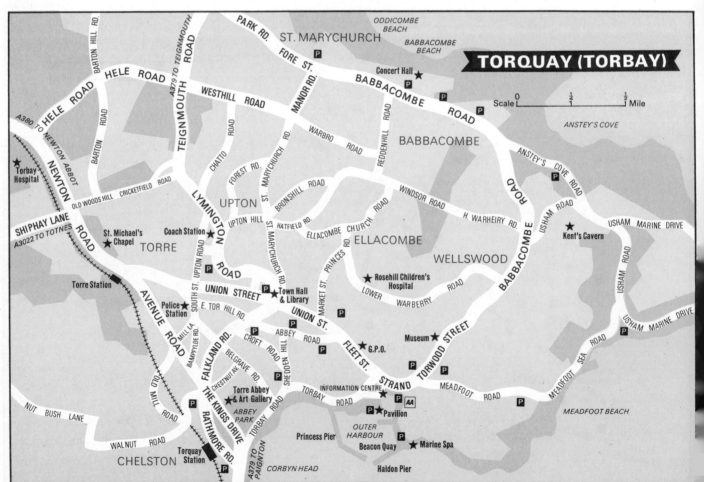

TORQUAY (TORBAY)

Scale 0 |_____| 1/4 |_____| 1/2 Mile

BARTON HILL RD.
PARK RD.
ST. MARYCHURCH
ODDICOMBE BEACH
HELE ROAD
FORE ST.
BABBACOMBE BEACH
A379 TO TEIGNMOUTH
WESTHILL ROAD
MANOR RD.
Concert Hall
BABBACOMBE ROAD
A380 TO NEWTON ABBOT
HELE ROAD
BARTON ROAD
TEIGNMOUTH ROAD
CHATTO ROAD
WARBRO ROAD
REDDENHILL ROAD
BABBACOMBE
ANSTEY'S COVE
ANSTEY'S COVE ROAD
Torbay Hospital
NEWTON ROAD
OLD WOODS HILL
CRICKETFIELD ROAD
FOREST RD.
ST. MARYCHURCH RD.
BRONSHILL ROAD
WINDSOR ROAD
UPTON
H. WARBERRY RD.
USHAM ROAD
USHAM MARINE DRIVE
SHIPHAY LANE
A3022 TO TOTNES
St. Michael's Chapel
Coach Station
LYMINGTON ROAD
UPTON HILL
ST. MARYCHURCH RD.
HATFIELD RD.
ELLACOMBE CHURCH ROAD
ELLACOMBE
WELLSWOOD
Kent's Cavern
USHAM ROAD
TORRE
PRINCES ST.
Rosehill Children's Hospital
LOWER WARBERRY ROAD
USHAM MARINE DRIVE
Torre Station
AVENUE ROAD
Police Station
UNION STREET
E. TOR HILL RD.
SOUTH ST.
Town Hall & Library
UNION ST.
MARKET ST.
Museum
TORWOOD STREET
MEADFOOT SEA ROAD
MILL LA.
BAMPFYLDE RD.
FALKLAND RD.
CROFT ROAD
ABBEY ROAD
SHEDEN HILL
FLEET ST.
G.P.O.
STRAND
MEADFOOT ROAD
NUT BUSH LANE
OLD MILL ROAD
BELGRAVE RD.
CHESTNUT AV.
Torre Abbey & Art Gallery
Information Centre
AA
Pavilion
MEADFOOT BEACH
THE KINGS DRIVE
RATHMORE RD.
ABBEY PARK
TORBAY ROAD
Princess Pier
OUTER HARBOUR
Beacon Quay
Marine Spa
CHELSTON
Torquay Station
A379 TO PAIGNTON
CORBYN HEAD
Haldon Pier

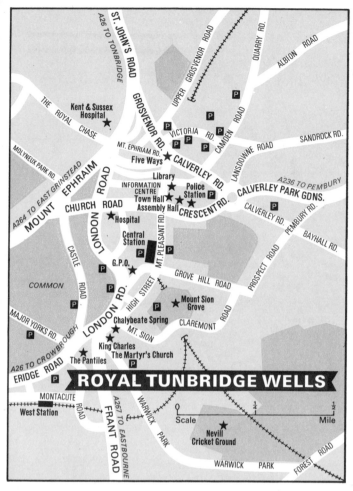

ROYAL TUNBRIDGE WELLS

Key locations (Royal Tunbridge Wells): ST. JOHN'S ROAD, A26 TO TONBRIDGE, UPPER GROSVENOR ROAD, GROSVENOR ROAD, QUARRY RD., ALBION ROAD, Kent & Sussex Hospital, THE ROYAL CHASE, VICTORIA RD., CAMDEN ROAD, SANDROCK RD., MT. EPHRIAM RD., Five Ways, CALVERLEY RD., LANSDOWNE ROAD, MOLYNEUX PARK RD., MOUNT EPHRAIM, Library, INFORMATION CENTRE, Town Hall, CHURCH ROAD, Police Station, CALVERLEY PARK GDNS., A236 TO PEMBURY, A264 TO EAST GRINSTEAD, Assembly Hall, Hospital, CRESCENT RD., CALVERLEY RD., PEMBURY RD., LONDON ROAD, Central Station, MT. PLEASANT RD., BAYHALL RD., CASTLE ROAD, G.P.O., PROSPECT ROAD, GROVE HILL ROAD, COMMON, HIGH STREET, Mount Sion Grove, MAJOR YORKS RD., Chalybeate Spring, MT. SION, CLAREMONT, A26 TO CROWBOROUGH, King Charles The Martyr's Church, The Pantiles, ERIDGE ROAD, MONTACUTE, West Station, A267 TO EASTBOURNE, WARWICK PARK, FRANT ROAD, Scale, Mile, Nevill Cricket Ground, FOREST ROAD

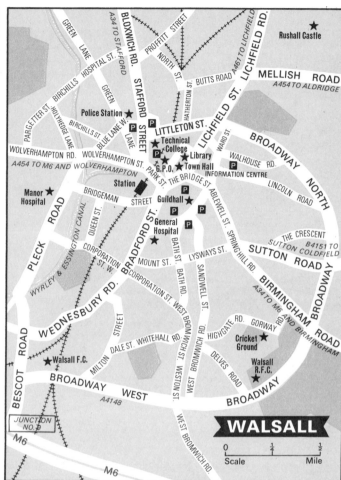

WALSALL

Key locations (Walsall): GREEN LANE, BLOXWICH RD., A34 TO STAFFORD, PROFFITT STREET, Rushall Castle, LICHFIELD RD., A461 TO LICHFIELD, MELLISH ROAD, A454 TO ALDRIDGE, STAFFORD STREET, NORTH ST., BUTTS ROAD, LITTLETON ST., LICHFIELD ST., BROADWAY NORTH, Police Station, PARGETTER ST., BIRCHILLS, HOSPITAL ST., HATHERTON ST., Technical College, Library, WARD ST., WALHOUSE RD., WOLVERHAMPTON RD., BLUE LANE W., G.P.O., Town Hall, INFORMATION CENTRE, A454 TO M6 AND WOLVERHAMPTON, WOLVERHAMPTON ST., PARK ST., THE BRIDGE ST., ABLEWELL ST., LINCOLN ROAD, Manor Hospital, Station, Guildhall, THE CRESCENT, B4151 TO SUTTON COLDFIELD, PLECK ROAD, BRIDGEMAN ST., BRADFORD ST., General Hospital, BATH ST., SPRINGHILL RD., SUTTON ROAD, WYRLEY & ESSINGTON CANAL, QUEEN ST., CORPORATION ST. W., Mount St., LYSWAYS ST., BIRMINGHAM ROAD, A34 TO M6 AND BIRMINGHAM, WEDNESBURY RD., CORPORATION ST., WEST BROMWICH ST., SANDWELL ST., HIGHGATE RD., GORWAY RD., Cricket Ground, BESCOT ROAD, STREET, MILTON DALE ST., WHITEHALL RD., WEST BROMWICH ST., WESTON ST., DELVES ROAD, Walsall R.F.C., Walsall F.C., BROADWAY WEST, A4148, WEST BROMWICH RD., BROADWAY, JUNCTION NO. 9, M6, Scale, Mile

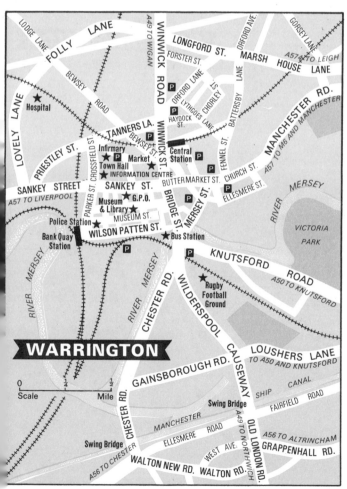

WARRINGTON

Key locations (Warrington): LODGE LANE, FOLLY LANE, WINWICK LANE, LONGFORD ST., MARSH HOUSE LANE, GORSEY LANE, A49 TO WIGAN, FORSTER ST., ORFORD AVE., A574 TO LEIGH, BEWSEY ROAD, WINWICK ROAD, ORFORD LANE, CHORLEY ST., BATTERSBY LANE, MANCHESTER RD., A57 TO M6 AND MANCHESTER, Hospital, LOVELY LANE, LYTHGOES LANE, HAYDOCK ST., TANNERS LA., BEWSEY ST., Infirmary, Market, Town Hall, Central Station, FENNEL ST., CHURCH ST., PRIESTLEY ST., CROSSFIELD ST., INFORMATION CENTRE, BUTTERMARKET ST., ELLESMERE ST., RIVER MERSEY, SANKEY STREET, A57 TO LIVERPOOL, PARKER ST., SANKEY ST., G.P.O., MERSEY ST., VICTORIA PARK, Museum & Library, MUSEUM ST., BRIDGE ST., Police Station, WILSON PATTEN ST., Bus Station, Bank Quay Station, KNUTSFORD ROAD, A50 TO KNUTSFORD, CHESTER RD., WILDERSPOOL CAUSEWAY, Rugby Football Ground, RIVER MERSEY, Scale, Mile, GAINSBOROUGH RD., LOUSHERS LANE TO A50 AND KNUTSFORD, MANCHESTER SHIP CANAL, Swing Bridge, FAIRFIELD ROAD, ELLESMERE ROAD, A56 TO ALTRINCHAM, A56 TO CHESTER, WALTON NEW RD., WALTON RD., WEST AVE., OLD LONDON RD., A49 TO NORTHWICH, GRAPPENHALL RD.

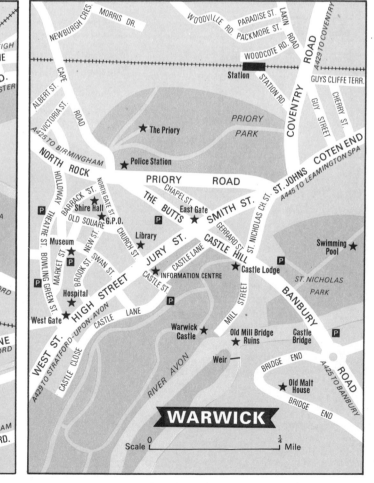

WARWICK

Key locations (Warwick): NEWBURGH CRES., MORRIS DR., WOODVILLE RD., PARADISE ST., PACKMORE ST., LAKIN ROAD, A429 TO COVENTRY, WOODCOTE RD., Station, STATON RD., COVENTRY ROAD, GUYS CLIFFE TERR., CAPE ROAD, ALBERT ST., VICTORIA ST., PRIORY PARK, The Priory, GUY STREET, CHERRY ST., COTEN END, A425 TO BIRMINGHAM, NORTH ROCK, Police Station, PRIORY ROAD, ST. JOHNS, A445 TO LEAMINGTON SPA, HOLLOWAY, CHAPEL ST., THE BUTTS, East Gate, SMITH ST., ST. NICHOLAS CH. ST., Shire Hall, NORTH GATE ST., Old Square, G.P.O., Library, JURY ST., CASTLE HILL, Swimming Pool, Museum, THEATRE ST., BARRACK ST., NEW ST., CHURCH ST., CASTLE ST., INFORMATION CENTRE, Castle Lodge, ST. NICHOLAS PARK, BOWLING GREEN ST., MARKET ST., BROOK ST., SWAN ST., CASTLE LANE, MILL STREET, Castle Hill, Hospital, HIGH STREET, West Gate, WEST ST., A429 TO STRATFORD-UPON-AVON, CASTLE CLOSE, Warwick Castle, Old Mill Bridge Ruins, Castle Bridge, BANBURY ROAD, A425 TO BANBURY, RIVER AVON, Weir, BRIDGE END, Old Malt House, BRIDGE END, Scale, Mile

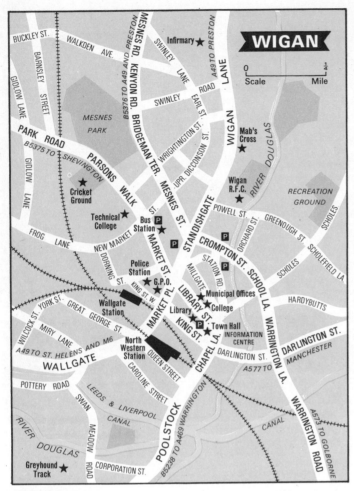

WIGAN

Scale 0 ¼ Mile

BUCKLEY ST.
WALKDEN AVE.
BARNSLEY STREET
GIDLOW LANE
MESNES RD. KENYON RD. AND PRESTON
B5376 TO 449 AND PRESTON
BRIDGEMAN TER.
SWINLEY LANE
SWINLEY
EARL ST.
WRIGHTINGTON ST.
WIGAN LANE
A49 TO PRESTON
Infirmary ★
Mab's Cross ★
Wigan R.F.C. ★
RIVER DOUGLAS
RECREATION GROUND
PARK ROAD
B5375 TO SHEVINGTON
PARSONS WALK
MESNES PARK
GIDLOW LANE
FROG LANE
Cricket Ground ★
Technical College ★
MESNES ST.
UPR. DICCONSON ST.
STANDISHGATE
POWELL ST.
CROMPTON ST.
ORCHARD ST.
SCHOOL LA.
GREENOUGH ST.
SCHOLEFIELD LA.
SCHOLES
Bus Station ★
NEW MARKET
DORNING ST.
MARKET ST.
MARKET PL.
KING ST. W.
STATION RD.
LIBRARY ST.
MILLGATE
Police Station ★
G.P.O. ★
Municipal Offices ★
College ★
Library ★
Town Hall ★ INFORMATION CENTRE
KING ST.
CHAPEL LA.
WARRINGTON LA.
HARDYBUTTS
Wallgate Station ★
WILCOCK ST.
YORK ST.
GREAT GEORGE ST.
MIRY LANE
A49 TO ST. HELENS AND M6
North Western Station ★
QUEEN STREET
WALLGATE
DARLINGTON ST.
A577 TO MANCHESTER
DARLINGTON ST.
A573 TO GOLBORNE
WARRINGTON ROAD
POTTERY ROAD
CAROLINE STREET
LEEDS & LIVERPOOL CANAL
SWAN MEADOW ROAD
POOLSTOCK
B5238 TO A469 WARRINGTON
CANAL
RIVER DOUGLAS
Greyhound Track ★
CORPORATION ST.

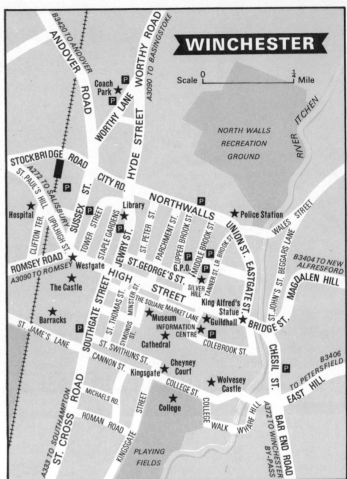

WINCHESTER

Scale 0 ¼ Mile

B3420 TO ANDOVER
ANDOVER ROAD
WORTHY LANE
WORTHY ROAD
HYDE STREET
A3090 TO BASINGSTOKE
RIVER ITCHEN
Coach Park ★
NORTH WALLS RECREATION GROUND
STOCKBRIDGE ROAD
A272 TO SALISBURY
ST. PAUL'S HILL
CITY RD.
NORTHWALLS
SUSSEX ST.
WALES STREET
Police Station ★
Hospital ★
CLIFTON TER.
UPR. HIGH ST.
TOWER ST.
ST. PETER ST.
STAPLE GARDENS
PARCHMENT ST.
UPPER BROOK ST.
MIDDLE BROOK ST.
LR. BROOK ST.
UNION ST.
EASTGATE ST.
ST. JOHN'S ST.
BEGGARS LANE
MAGDALEN HILL
B3404 TO NEW ALRESFORD
ROMSEY ROAD
A3090 TO ROMSEY
Westgate ★
JEWRY ST.
ST. GEORGE'S ST.
G.P.O.
TANNER ST.
SILVER HILL
King Alfred's Statue ★
BRIDGE ST.
The Castle ★
HIGH STREET
ST. THOMAS ST.
THE SQUARE
MARKET LANE
Museum ★
INFORMATION CENTRE
Guildhall ★
COLEBROOK ST.
CHESIL ST.
B3406 TO PETERSFIELD
Barracks ★
SOUTHGATE STREET
ST. JAME'S LANE
SYMONDS ST.
ST. SWITHUNS ST.
Cathedral ★
CANNON ST.
Cheyney Court ★
Kingsgate ★
Wolvesey Castle ★
COLLEGE ST.
EAST HILL
A333 TO SOUTHAMPTON
ST. CROSS ROAD
MICHAELS RD.
ROMAN ROAD
KINGSGATE STREET
College ★
COLLEGE WALK
WHARF HILL
BAR END ROAD
A272 TO WINCHESTER BY-PASS
PLAYING FIELDS

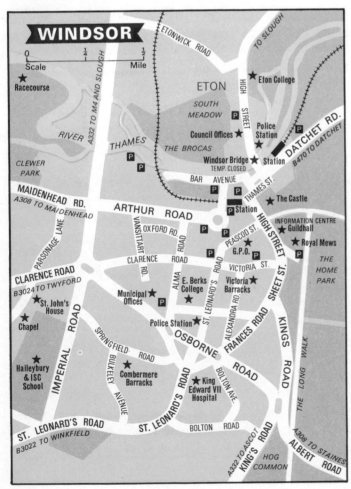

WINDSOR

Scale 0 ¼ ½ Mile

ETONWICK ROAD
TO SLOUGH
Racecourse ★
ETON
SOUTH MEADOW
HIGH STREET
Eton College ★
A332 TO M4 AND SLOUGH
RIVER THAMES
CLEWER PARK
THE BROCAS
Council Offices ★
Police Station ★
DATCHET RD.
B470 TO DATCHET
Windsor Bridge ★ TEMP. CLOSED
Station ★
BAR AVENUE
MAIDENHEAD RD.
A308 TO MAIDENHEAD
ARTHUR ROAD
THAMES ST.
Station ★
VANSITTART RD.
OXFORD RD.
PEASCOD ST.
The Castle ★
PARSONAGE LANE
CLARENCE ROAD
CLARENCE RD.
ROAD
G.P.O. ★
HIGH STREET
INFORMATION CENTRE
Guildhall ★
Royal Mews ★
CLARENCE ROAD
B3024 TO TWYFORD
St. John's House ★
Chapel ★
ALMA ROAD
E. Berks College ★
VICTORIA ST.
Victoria Barracks ★
SHEET ST.
THE HOME PARK
Municipal Offices ★
ST. LEONARD'S ROAD
Police Station ★
ALEXANDRA RD.
FRANCES ROAD
KINGS ROAD
Haileybury & ISC School ★
IMPERIAL ROAD
SPRINGFIELD ROAD
BULKELEY AVENUE
Combermere Barracks ★
OSBORNE ROAD
King Edward VII Hospital ★
BOLTON AVE.
THE LONG WALK
ST. LEONARD'S ROAD
B3022 TO WINKFIELD
ST. LEONARD'S ROAD
BOLTON ROAD
KING'S ROAD
A332 TO ASCOT
A308 TO STAINES
ALBERT ROAD
HOG COMMON

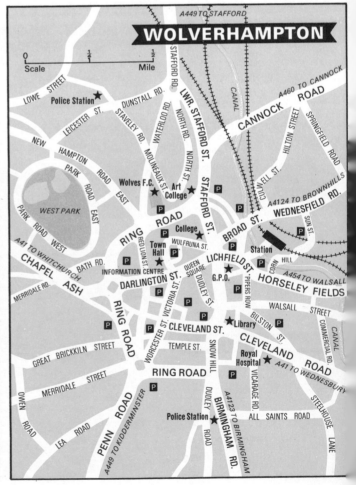

WOLVERHAMPTON

Scale 0 ¼ ½ Mile

A449 TO STAFFORD
STAFFORD RD.
LWR. STAFFORD ST.
CANAL
A460 TO CANNOCK
CANNOCK ROAD
LOWE STREET
Police Station ★
LEICESTER ST.
DUNSTALL RD.
STAVELEY RD.
WATERLOO RD.
NORTH RD.
NORTH RD.
HILTON STREET
SPRINGFIELD ROAD
A4124 TO BROWNHILLS
NEW HAMPTON ROAD EAST
MOLINEAUX ST.
Wolves F.C. ★
Art College ★
STAFFORD ST.
WEDNESFIELD ROAD
WEST PARK
PARK ROAD EAST
CLWELL ST.
College ★
BROAD ST.
Station ★
RING ROAD
WULFRUNA ST.
CORN HILL
A454 TO WALSALL
A41 TO WHITCHURCH
BATH RD.
Town Hall ★
LICHFIELD ST.
HORSELEY FIELDS
CHAPEL ASH
INFORMATION CENTRE
Queen Square
PIPERS ROW
WALSALL STREET
COMMERCIAL RD.
MERRIDALE RD.
DARLINGTON ST.
VICTORIA ST.
DUDLEY ST.
G.P.O. ★
BILSTON ST.
CANAL
RING ROAD
WORCESTER ST.
Library ★
CLEVELAND ST.
CLEVELAND ROAD
GREAT BRICKKILN STREET
TEMPLE ST.
SNOW HILL
Royal Hospital ★
VICARAGE RD.
A41 TO WEDNESBURY
MERRIDALE STREET
RING ROAD
A41 TO KIDDERMINSTER
PENN ROAD
A449 TO KIDDERMINSTER
OWEN ROAD
LEA ROAD
DUDLEY RD.
Police Station ★
BIRMINGHAM RD.
A4123 TO BIRMINGHAM
ALL SAINTS ROAD
STEELHOUSE LANE

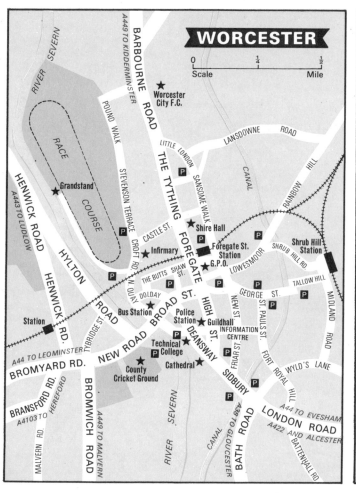

WORCESTER

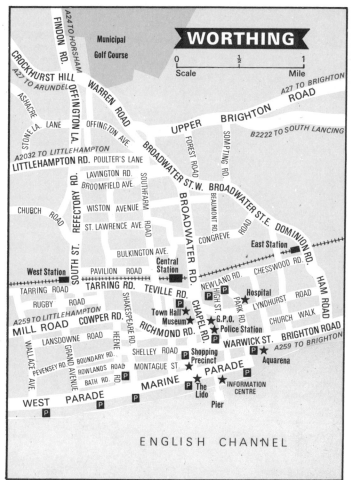

WORTHING

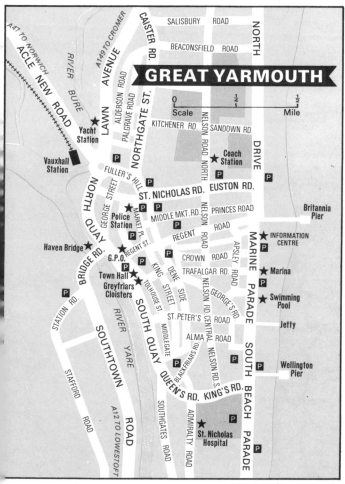

GREAT YARMOUTH

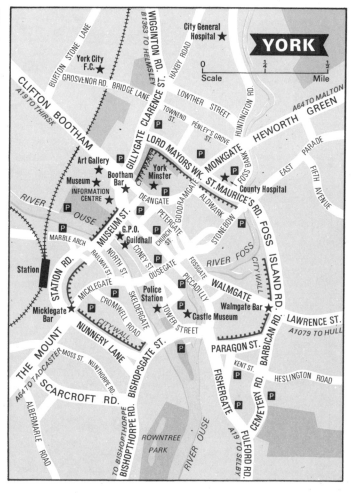

YORK

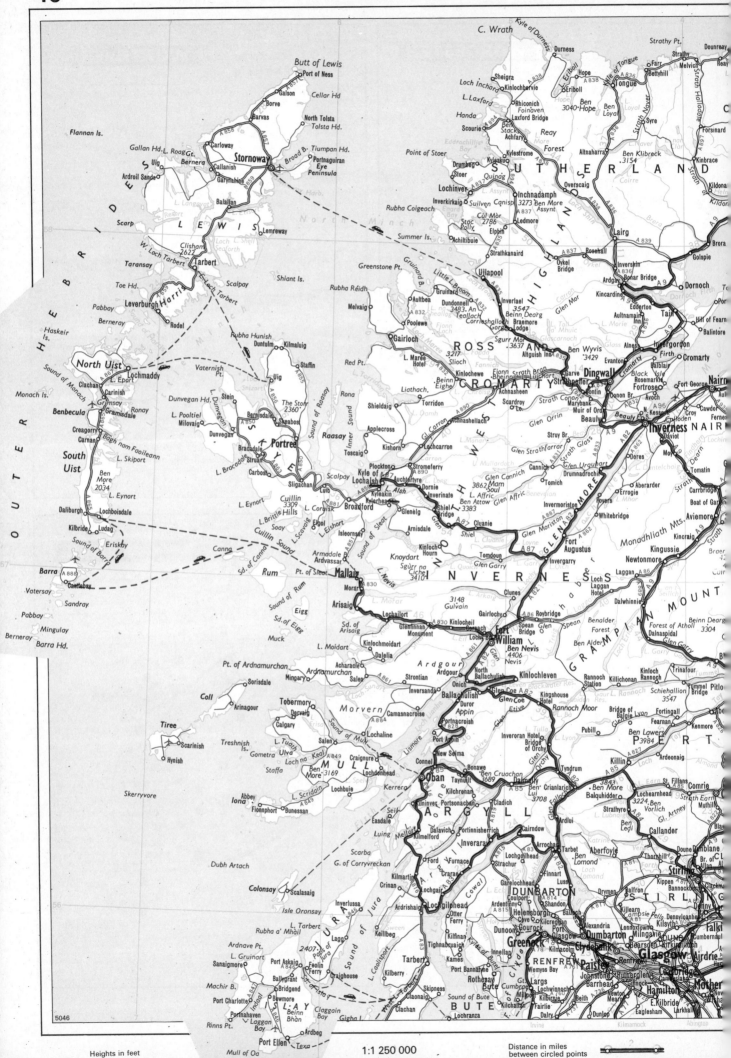

CAITHNESS (inset — top left)

Stromness · Dunnet B. · Dunnet · Mey · John o' Groats · Duncansby Hd.
Castletown · Keiss · A9 · Reiss · A882 · Sinclair's B. · Noss Hd.
Hakirk · Watten · **Wick**
THNESS
Latheron · A895 · Lybster
Dunbeath
Berriedale
lmsdale

ORKNEY (inset — top centre)

Mull Head · North Ronaldsay
Westray · Pierowall · The North Sd. · Nth. Ronaldsay Firth
Rapness · Overbister · **Sanday**
Brough Hd. · Rousay · Eday · Backaland · Sanday Sd.
The Barony · Marwick Hd. · Brinyan · Egilsay · Whitehall · **Stronsay**
Skara Brae · Dounbay · Stronsay · **Shapinsay** · Auskerry
L. o' Stenness · Balfour · Firth
Kirkwall · Skaill
Stromness · **Mainland** · St. Mary's · Copinsay
Graemsay · Ward Hill 1565' · **Hoy**
Rora Hd. · Lyness · St. Margaret's Hope
Wateringhouse · **South Ronaldsay**
Pentland Firth · Burwick · Brough Ness
Dunnet Head · Stroma
Scrabster · John o' Groats

ZETLAND (SHETLAND) (inset — right)

Muckle Flugga · Herma Ness · Burra Firth
Haroldswick · Norwick
Baltasound · Balta
Cullivoe · **Unst** · A968 · Uyeasound · Uyea
Dalsetter · Gutcher · Belmont
Yell Sound · Isbister · Fetlar
South-haa · **Yell** · W. Sandwick · Funzie
The Faither · North Collafirth · Otterswick Sd.
Esha Ness · Hillswick · Ollaberry · A970 · Burravoe
Stenness · Mossbank · Heoga Ness
St. Magnus Bay · Scatsta
Muckle Roe · Brae · Lunna · Out Skerries
Papa Stour · Laxo · Whalsey
Sandness · Voe · Dury Voe
Walls · **Mainland** · Aith
Vaila · Tresta · I. of Noss
Reawick · **Lerwick**
Ham · Foula · Scalloway · Bressay · Bressay Sd.
Hamnavoe · Cuningsburgh
West Burra · Sandwick · Mousa
Scousburgh
Cliff Sd.
Fitful Head · A970
Tolob · Sumburgh Head
Sumburgh

Stonybreck · **Fair Isle** · Aberdeen · Lerwick

MAIN MAP

Lossiemouth · Hopeman · Portknockie · Rosehearty · **Fraserburgh**
ourghead · Findochty · Portsoy · Banff · Macduff · Inverallochy
Elgin · Barmouth · Portgordon · **Buckie** · Cullen · Gardenstown · Rattray Hd.
Kinloss · Llanbryde · Mosstodloch · Fochabers · A98 · Strichen · A952
Rafford · Dallas · Fife Keith · Aberchirder · New Pitsligo · Mintlaw · **Peterhead**
MORAY · Rothes · Keith · A96 · Cuminestown · Maud · A950 · Longside
Archiestown · Craigellachie · Turriff · New Deer · Boddam
Knockando · Dufftown · **Huntly** · Rhynie · Rothienorman · Fyvie · Methlick · Hatton
Ballindalloch · Aberlour · Cabrach · Oldmeldrum · Tarves · Ellon · Cruden Bay
Tomnavoulin · **BANFF** · Oyne · A96 · Pitmedden · A952
Knockandhu · Tomintoul · Bridge of Alford · **Inverurie** · Kintore · Newburgh
Alford · Kemnay · Balmedie
Cock Bridge · Strathdon · **ABERDEEN**
Glen Avon · Tarland · Dunecht · Skene · **Aberdeen** · Girdle Ness
Macdui · Morven 2862 · Torphins · Peterculter
Braemar · Crathie · **Ballater** · Aboyne · **Banchory** · Muchalls
Inver · Balmoral Castle · Strachan · **Stonehaven**
Lochnagar 3786 · **KINCARDINE** · Mt Keen 3077 · Cairn o' Mount 1488
An Socach · Glas Maol · Tarfside · Fordoun · Inverbervie
vil's Elbow · Glen Clova · Clova · Fettercairn · Gourdon
Spittal of Glenshee · Edzell · **Laurencekirk**
kie · Glenisla · Dykehead · Marykirk · St. Cyrus
michael · Kirriemuir · **ANGUS** · Tannadice · Brechin · **Montrose**
inluig · Br. of Cally · Alyth · Friockheim · Lunan B. · Inverkeilor
Blairgowrie · Glamis · **Forfar**
Birnam · Newtyle · **Arbroath**
Meikleour · Coupar Angus · Monifieth · Carnoustie
kfoot · Stanley · **Dundee** · Broughty Ferry · Buddon Ness · Bell Rock
New Scone · Tayport · Newport on Tay
Perth · Errol · Wormit · Leuchars
Glencarse · Newburgh · **St. Andrews**
Bridge of Earn · Abernethy · Cupar · Dairsie · Pitscottie · Fife Ness
rarder · Auchtermuchty · Ceres · Largoward · Crail
Glenfarg · Strathmiglo · **FIFE** · Kilrenny · I. of May
Milnathort · Falkland · Lundin Links · Anstruther
KIN · Glenrothes · Leslie · Largo · Pittenweem
Kinross · Markinch · Leven · St. Monance
Rumblingbridge · Whigstreet · Buckhaven and Methil
Lochgelly
Cowdenbeath · **Kirkcaldy**
unfermline · Kinghorn · Bass Rock
mouth · Inverkeithing · Burntisland · North Berwick
Rosyth · Inchkeith · Aberlady · **Dunbar**
Queensferry · Gullane · A198
Leith · Musselburgh · Prestonpans · E. Linton · St. Abb's Hd.
Edinburgh · Haddington · Cockburnspath · St. Abb's
Kirkliston · Dalkeith · **EAST LOTHIAN** · Gifford · Coldingham · Eyemouth
THIAN · Balerno · Newtongrange · Lammermuir Hills · Ayton
MIDLOTHIAN · Loanhead · Penicuik · Preston · Swinside
own · West · Carlops · South · Duns · Paxton
Linton · Moorfoot Hills · Carfraemill · **Berwick-upon-Tweed**
Eddleston · **BERWICK** · Westruther · Tweedmouth
Ahington · Greenlaw · Lauder · Alnwick · Galashiels

NORTH SEA

0 · 10 · 20 · 30 · 40 · 50 Miles
0 · 10 · 20 · 30 · 40 · 50 · 60 · 70 · 80 Kilometres

John Bartholomew & Son Ltd

| 0 | 10 | 20 | 30 | 40 | 50 Miles |
| 0 | 10 | 20 | 30 | 40 | 50 | 60 | 70 | 80 Kilometres |

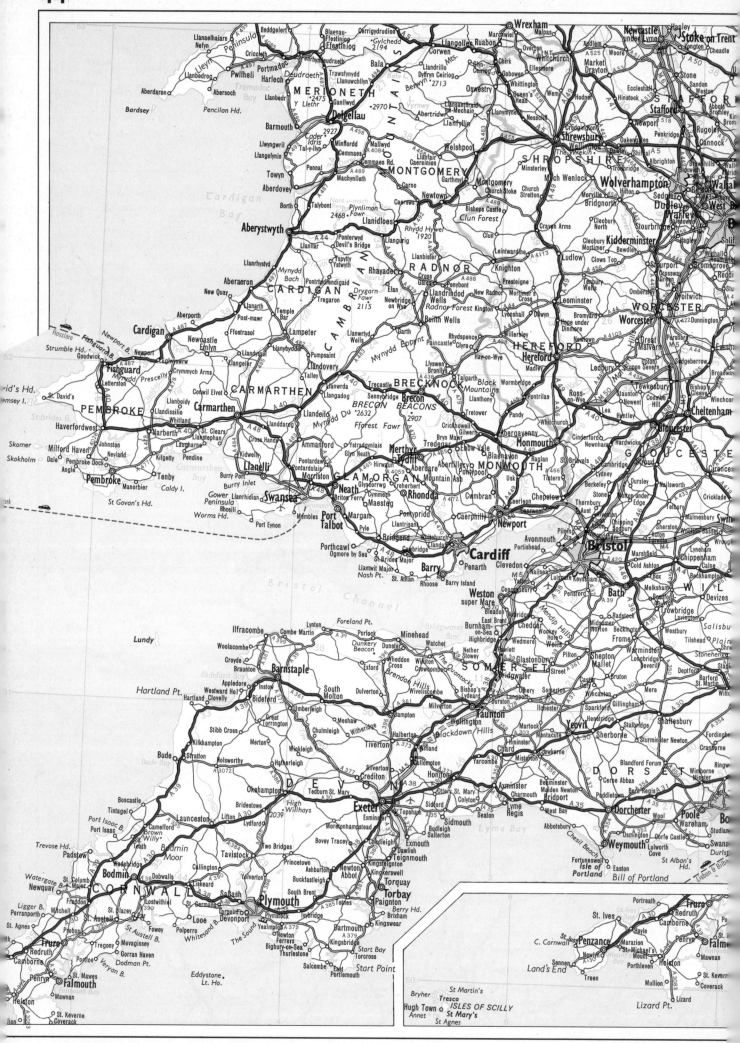

Distances in miles between circled points

1:1 250 000

Heights in feet

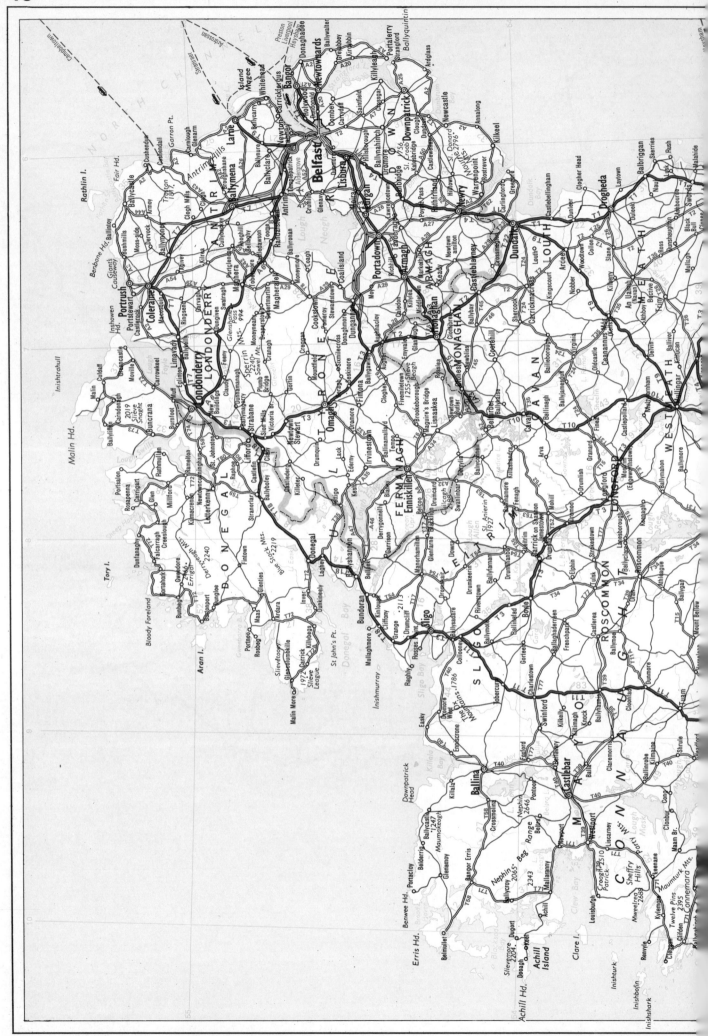

Distances in miles
between circled points

1:1 250 000

Heights in feet

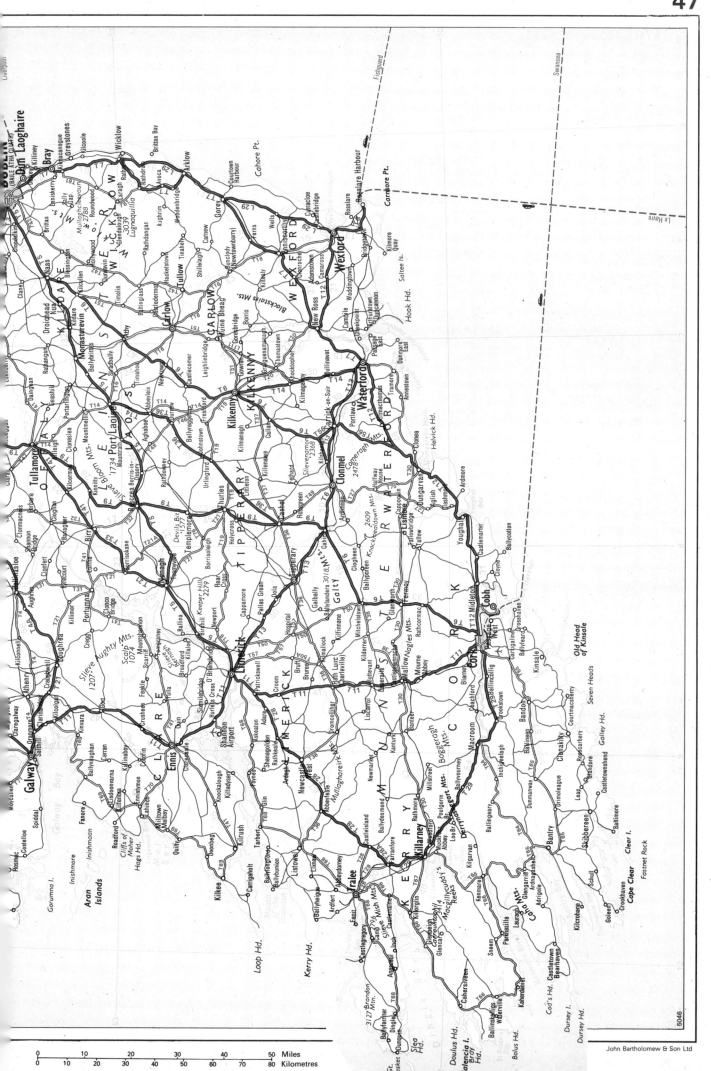

0   10   20   30   40   50 Miles
0   10   20   30   40   50   60   70   80 Kilometres

INDEX 48

Town Plans drawn by F.H. Reitz, M.S.I.A.

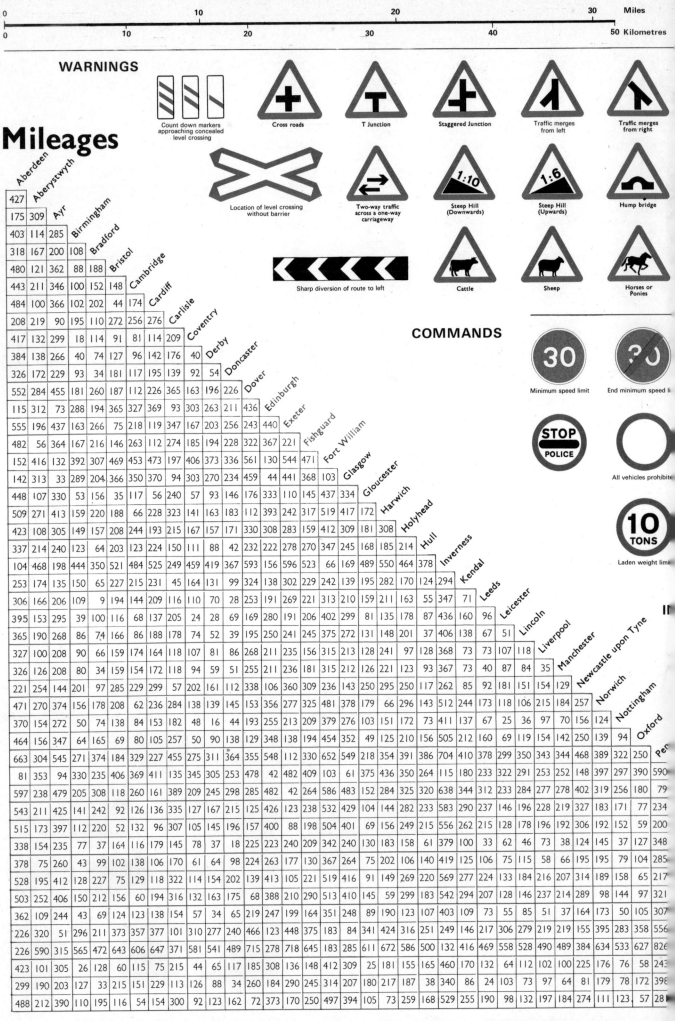

Distances assume the use of ferries where appropriate